Berlitz

DUBAI

POCKET GUIDE

Walking Eye
mobile app

Discover the world's best destinations with the Insight Guides Walking Eye app, available to download for free in the App Store and Google Play.

The container app provides easy access to fantastic free content on events and activities taking place in your current location or chosen destination, with the possibility of booking, as well as the regularly-updated Insight Guides travel blog: Inspire Me. In addition, you can purchase curated, premium destination guides through the app, which feature local highlights, hotel, bar, restaurant and shopping listings, an A to Z of practical information and more. Or purchase and download Insight Guides eBooks straight to your device.

Download on the **App Store**   GET IT ON **Google Play**

TOP 10 ATTRACTIONS

BURJ AL ARAB
The 'seven-star' hotel is the city's architectural icon. See page 68.

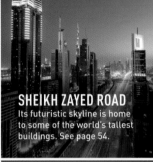

SHEIKH ZAYED ROAD
Its futuristic skyline is home to some of the world's tallest buildings. See page 54.

THE GOLD SOUK
Pick up a glittering souvenir of Dubai in this world-famous shopping quarter. See page 41.

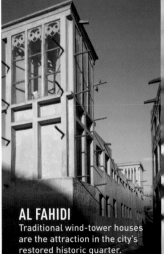

AL FAHIDI
Traditional wind-tower houses are the attraction in the city's restored historic quarter. See page 36.

MALL TIME
Max out your credit cards at Dubai's dazzling array of shopping malls. See page 59.

ABRAS (WATER TAXIS)
Enjoy a ride between the traditional souks on either side of Dubai Creek. See page 38.

DESERT SAFARI
Head out into the desert for an exhilarating 4x4 ride across the dunes. See page 125.

MADINAT JUMEIRAH
A fabulous re-creation of old Arabia, with souks, restaurants, cafés and canals. See page 69.

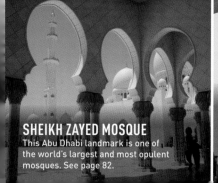

SHEIKH ZAYED MOSQUE
This Abu Dhabi landmark is one of the world's largest and most opulent mosques. See page 82.

DOWNTOWN DUBAI
A clutch of record-breaking attractions centred on the extraordinary Burj Khalifa, the world's tallest building. See page 57.

A PERFECT DAY

9.00am

Gold and spices

After breakfast in your hotel, head to the glittering Gold Souk in Deira, exploring the gold shops and adjacent Spice Souk, perhaps combined with a visit to the nearby Al Ahmadiya School and Heritage House.

1.00pm

Wind towers

Head down to the atmospheric Al Fahidi Historical Neighbourhood, with its marvellous old wind-towered houses, and grab a bite to eat at the beautiful XVA Café and Gallery.

12.00pm

Historical interlude

Spend an hour exploring the excellent Dubai Museum – an essential point of reference for anyone interested in the city's past.

2.00pm

Into the new city

Catch a cab or take the metro for the short journey south to the spectacular skyscrapers of Sheikh Zayed Road. Get out at the iconic Emirates Tower and walk down the strip, admiring the eclectic high-rise architecture en route.

11.00am

Along the Creek

Hop on an abra for the five-minute ride across the Creek to Bur Dubai, and walk along the waterfront to Shindagha for views of Old Dubai. Retrace your steps back through the souk to emerge by the Juma Grand Mosque and Dubai Museum.

IN DUBAI

3.30pm

Up to the top

Exit through the back of the Dubai Mall to reach the heart of the Downtown Dubai development, with the Dubai Fountain in front of you and the huge Burj Khalifa, the world's tallest building, to your right. Head into the Burj and ride a high-speed elevator up to the At The Top observation deck (you will need to have booked this in advance) for sweeping views of the city.

2.30pm

Shopping

From the bottom of Sheikh Zayed Road bear left down Financial Centre Road to reach the main entrance to Dubai Mall. Spend some time here browsing the shops, visiting the in-house aquarium or going for a spin on the ice rink.

7.00pm

Arabian night

There is a vast range of superb places to eat all around the Madinat Jumeirah – the canalside venues are particularly lively after dark and a great place to people-watch. After dinner, catch a tram for the short trip down to the One&Only Royal Mirage hotel and head for the gorgeous little Rooftop Bar, which often has a DJ later on.

4.30pm

Sail of the century

Catch a cab and head down to the stunning Madinat Jumeirah complex, explore the Madinat's souk, canals and shops, and then enjoy the unforgettable views of the sail-shaped Burj Al Arab next door over a sundowner at the Bahri Bar.

CONTENTS

INTRODUCTION

Nowhere is quite like Dubai. In the space of barely four decades, the city has transformed itself from a modest Arabian trading town, which few outside the region had ever heard of, into one of the planet's most glamorous, futuristic and talked-about destinations, home to the world's tallest building, its biggest shopping mall, its largest man-made island and a host of other record-busting developments – all of which continue to attract hyperbole, admiration and derision in equal measure.

DUBAI PAST AND PRESENT

Modern Dubai's go-for-it dynamism is nothing new and the city has always boasted an entrepreneurial spirit and ability to seize whatever opportunities it has been presented with. As early as 1894, Sheikh Maktoum Bin Hasher al Maktoum was enticing merchants from Iran and India to settle in the city with the promise of zero taxation, establishing the basis of the modern city's cosmopolitan, business-friendly orientation. Old Dubai was a flourishing port long before oil was discovered in the emirate in 1966, at various times making a living out of a vibrant trade in pearls and gold (often smuggled), as well as other commercial activities.

The development of modern Dubai was kick-started by the discovery of oil in the 1960s, although Dubai's oil reserves have only ever been relatively modest. Oil production peaked at 410,000 barrels a day in 1991 and has been in decline ever since.

However, oil revenues provided the money to construct a modern industrial infrastructure, supervised by the canny Sheikh Rashid, who laid the foundations for the city's current prosperity. Rashid's son, Sheikh Mohammed, the current ruler of Dubai,

The iconic Burj Al Arab Hotel sits on a man-made island

has further accelerated the pace of diversification, overseeing the construction of lavish tourist facilities alongside a string of business-friendly initiatives ranging from assorted free-trade and enterprise zones such as Jebel Ali Port, Dubai Internet and Media cities, and the Dubai International Financial Centre (DIFC), all of which are aimed at positioning Dubai as the tourist, business and financial capital of the Middle East. Major global players have relocated their regional offices to Dubai, pushing the number of nationalities resident in the city to over 200 and the overall population to 3.1 million (up from under 700,000 in 1995). Foreigners now outnumber native Emiratis by more than ten to one, giving the city its extraordinarily multicultural and cosmopolitan flavour.

Not surprisingly, there have been growing pains along the way. Exploitation and alleged human-rights abuses of low-paid workers brought from India and Pakistan to labour on the city's endless construction sites have proved a running sore on the city's

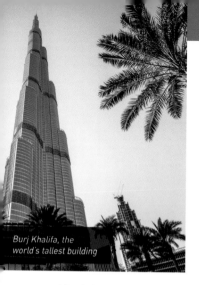

Burj Khalifa, the
world's tallest building

image. Social tensions between the many different nationalities cohabiting within the city also continue to provoke friction, while the regular incarceration of visiting Westerners on charges ranging from carrying drugs to kissing in public has generated endless critical column inches overseas. Environmental concerns associated with Dubai's breakneck development are another major problem, while the city's creaking infrastructure, with inadequate public transport and horrific traffic jams, hasn't helped either, although the opening of the superb Metro and tram services have at least gone some way towards addressing the latter problem. Worst of all was the 2008 credit crunch, during which the city teetered dangerously on the edge of bankruptcy before being rescued by oil-rich Abu Dhabi.

As a result many of the city's more outrageous projects were cancelled, or put on hold, including the artificial archipelagos of the World and the Universe, the Arabian Canal, and Jumeirah Garden City. As the property market picked up, however, work resumed on various developments, including Business Bay, a new business district along the extension of Dubai Creek, which was inaugurated in 2016.

The city continues to look towards the future with renewed, if cautious, optimism, while also preparing to host the World Expo 2020, where it hopes to astonish the world once again.

BEACHES AND SHOPPING

Modern Dubai's attempt to conquer the global tourist market is based on a wide range of attractions. For visitors wanting a weekend stopover with sun and sand en route Dubai provides the perfect choice, although equally, you could spend weeks here, exploring the city's myriad attractions and other sights across the UAE. The weather, too, is a major draw. Dubai is blessed with 12 months of sunshine, and although summer temperatures can reach punishing extremes, from October to May Dubai's deliciously Mediterranean climate offers the perfect respite for sun-starved Europeans and North Americans.

Sweeping beaches and some of the planet's most lavish and memorable hotels are also an attraction, while the city's outstanding range of top-notch bars and restaurants add to the appeal, as do the extensive shopping opportunities scattered about the city, centred on some of the world's largest and most spectacular

⊙ EMIRATI DRESS

UAE national dress is worn in the workplace, at home and when out and about. The men's white, floor-length robe is known as the *kandoora* or *dishdasha*. The cloth headdress, which can be white, or red-and-white check, is a *gutra* secured by a stiff black cord known as an *agal*, with which Emiratis' *bedu* ancestors hobbled their camels' legs. Increasingly among young men, baseball caps are replacing the *gutra* and *agal*. The most visible items of women's clothing are the floor-length black cloak, the *abaya* and the headscarf, called a *sheyla*. Older women may be seen wearing the stiff gold and lacquer face mask known as a *burqa*, though this is increasingly rare. Children are often dressed in Western-style clothes.

malls, many of which rank as tourist attractions in their own right. The city's magnificent modern architecture is also guaranteed to dazzle – Dubai is, after all, now home to the world's tallest building, and boasts more and bigger skyscrapers per square mile than anywhere else on the planet. And then there are the old city's attractions: traditional buildings with their distinctive wind-towers and sandy courtyards, the bustling souks of Deira and Bur Dubai and the Creek itself, at the heart of the old city, which is still busy day and night with traditional wooden *abras* and trading dhows, offering a living link with the Dubai of a century past.

LAYOUT OF THE CITY

Dubai is the second largest of the seven emirates that comprise the United Arab Emirates (UAE). Located northeast of the federal capital, Abu Dhabi, on the southern shores of the Arabian Gulf, Dubai faces Iran and has an eastern land border with Oman. The emirate covers 3,885 sq km (1,500 sq miles) of flat coastal plain and rolling desert dunes, with barren mountains, the Hajar range, in the distant east around the Dubai enclave of Hatta.

The modern city is extremely linear, stretching for over 20km (12 miles) from the old city-centre districts of Bur Dubai and Deira, on either side of the Creek, down to Dubai Marina in the south. The Sheikh Zayed Road runs the length of the city, connecting the various districts and continuing to Abu Dhabi.

Transport within the city has been revolutionized over the past few years following the opening of the Dubai Metro, which provides a cheap and convenient way of making trips across the city, and with the inauguration of the first tram line in 2014. New Metro lines and planned extensions should further improve matters. For now, however, most residents continue to get around by car, and traffic jams are an established fact of city life.

A BRIEF HISTORY

The location of what is now the United Arab Emirates (UAE), straddling trade routes between the ancient civilisations of southern Mesopotamia (present-day Iraq) and the Indus Valley, and later between Europe and the Eastern colonies, ensured that the region has welcomed, traded with and been influenced by foreign visitors for several millennia.

The area that today comprises the UAE and northern Oman has been known by various names throughout history. To the Sumerians of southern Mesopotamia it was Magan, famous for its copper in the 3rd millennium BC. To the Persians of the 1st millennium BC, Magan was Maka, which they incorporated into their empire in the 6th century BC. The Roman-era Greek historian and geographer Strabo of Amaseia (c.64BC–AD21) referred to the coast as the 'promontory of the Macae in Arabia'. To the Persian Sassanids of the 3rd to the 7th century AD it was Mazun, the 27th land of their empire. From the 4th century AD to the Islamic conquest of the 7th century, a significant number of its Sassanid-era inhabitants were Christians. The early church knew the UAE coast as Bet Mazunaye, and

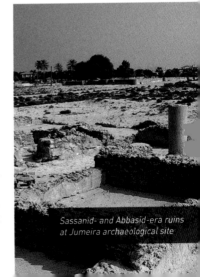

Sassanid- and Abbasid-era ruins at Jumeira archaeological site

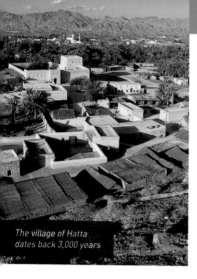
The village of Hatta dates back 3,000 years

established monasteries along it. One of these, on Sir Bani Yas island in the emirate of Abu Dhabi, has been excavated and preserved.

EARLY CIVILISATION

Though there are several important archaeological sites within Dubai's city limits, much of what we know about the region's early history comes from finds made since the late 1950s at other UAE sites. The earliest evidence of human habitation is a dwelling in Dalma, Abu Dhabi, dating back 6,000 years. Subsequent discoveries of prehistoric painted pottery pieces in the northern emirates of Sharjah, Umm Al Qaiwain and Ras Al Khaimah suggest that some form of international trade existed between the inhabitants of the coastal villages and the pre-Sumerian Ubaid civilisation, which flourished in southern Mesopotamia from 5600 to 3900BC. Also in Umm Al Qaiwain, archaeological evidence suggests a pearl trade existed in the 5th millennium BC.

One of the most famous archaeological sites in the UAE is Umm an Nar (meaning 'Mother of Fire'), near Abu Dhabi, a 3rd-millennium BC Bronze Age settlement that has given its name to the period in UAE history between 2700 and 2000BC. Camel bones found here and dated to 2500–2200BC are thought to be the earliest evidence in the world for the domestication of this animal.

A significant Umm an Nar-era site in Dubai is at Al Sufouh, between Jumeira and the Dubai Marina. In the early 1990s, a circular Umm an Nar-type tomb and settlement was excavated here.

IRON AGE

During the Iron Age, between 1200 and 300BC, the population of the Emirates would have been the largest up to that point in its history. Numerous mud-brick villages of the period unearthed by archaeologists include Al Qusais in Dubai, which is probably the site of a resettled Bronze Age community.

During the Hellenistic era, from around 300BC to a century or so after the time of Christ, two of the most important cities were Mleiha, south of Dhaid in Sharjah emirate and Ad-Dour, near Umm Al Qaiwain, which is the largest pre-Islamic site on the Gulf coast. Finds at these locations include Greek pottery, wine-jar handles from Rhodes and Roman glass. Aramaic lettering on much of the coinage found at Mleiha and Ad-Dour, as well as on stone and bronze inscriptions, indicates that the language of Christ was the lingua franca of the region in the pre-Islamic era.

In the late Sassanid era, a pre-Islamic trading post – a stop on the trade route between Mesopotamia and Oman – was established in what is now the Jumeira district of Dubai. Excavations have revealed the foundations of a Sassanid governor's palace, houses built of beach rock (farush) covered with lime plaster, and a marketplace. The settlement was subsequently expanded by the Abbasids in the early Islamic era. As a hub for East–West trade, under first the Sassanids then the Abbasids, Jumeira would have seen luxuries

What's in a name

In Arabic names, 'Bin' and 'Ibn' both mean 'son of': Mohammed Bin Rashid is Mohammed, son of Rashid. 'Bint' is 'daughter of'.

such as copper, spices, frankincense, sandalwood and teak move west, probably by sea, and valuable cargoes of gold, silver and textiles heading in the other direction.

ISLAMIC ERA TO COLONIAL PERIOD

Arabic replaced Aramaic after the region converted to Islam in AD632. The first of the Muslim Arab dynasties was the Umayyad Caliphate, which ruled in Damascus from 661. In 749, the rival Abbasids seized power and began to exert their influence in the area, as evidenced by the early Islamic-era additions to the trading post in Jumeira, the architecture of which reflects the Abbasid style.

In the late Islamic era, thanks to the skills of Arabic navigators such as Ibn Majid, inhabitants of the region traded with East Africa, and as far as India and China, as revealed by discoveries of fine Chinese porcelain fragments at coastal sites.

The earliest certain reference to 'Dibei' was made in 1580 by the Venetian court jeweller Gasparo Balbi, who was drawn to the region by the quality of its pearls.

In the 19th century, the British asserted their control of the trade route to colonial India through a series of treaties with local rulers. One of these was Mohammed Bin Hazza, who ruled the small fishing and pearling village of Dubai from his Creekside Shindagha home at the time of an 1820 agreement. A British understanding with Hazza led to the first recognition on paper that Dubai was an entity separate from communities of Abu Dhabi and Sharjah.

THE MAKTOUM ERA

Dubai's modern history really begins in 1833, with the arrival of the Maktoum family and around 800 of their followers, who had left their homes in Abu Dhabi in disgust at the repressive behaviour of the then ruler. Installed in Dubai, Sheikh Maktoum bin Buti took over control of the town, inaugurating the Maktoum family dynasty, which survives to this day.

The position of the Maktoums was initially precarious, wedged between the two far more powerful emirates of Abu Dhabi and Sharjah, although the signing of a further treaty with the British in 1835 afforded them some measure of security. Pearling continued to be the mainstay of the town's economy, while seaborne trade through Dubai also flourished, the souk expanded, and in 1841 the new settlement of Deira was established on the opposite side of the Creek. British influence continued to grow, resulting in further treaties including, most importantly, the 1892 Exclusive Agreement, whereby Dubai agreed to hand over all its foreign policy affairs to Britain in return for a guarantee of protection – an agreement which was to remain in force until Independence in 1971.

IRANIAN INFLUENCE

Another result of British influence was the arrival of the first Indian merchants in the emirate – the beginnings of what would later become a large community of Indian settlers. The Indians were not the only foreigners to start settling in Dubai. Of far more immediate importance was the arrival of large numbers of Iranian traders during the

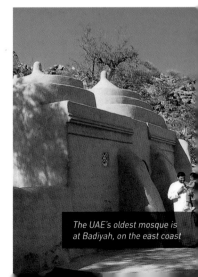

The UAE's oldest mosque is at Badiyah, on the east coast

1890s. Increasingly punitive taxes in the flourishing Iranian port of Lingah across the Gulf came to the attention of Dubai ruler Sheikh Maktoum bin Hasher (who ruled from 1894 to 1906), who sent emissaries to Lingah to invite the unhappy merchants to Dubai, promising them free land and zero taxation. The Iranians arrived in their hundreds, providing a huge boost to the economy of the city and providing another cosmopolitan twist to the local population, as well as building the marvellous cluster of wind-towered houses, which can still be seen in Bastakiya. Dubai continues to enjoy close links with Iran to this day, much to the displeasure of the USA, and indeed of the federal government in Abu Dhabi.

SHEIKH RASHID

Dubai continued to flourish during the first decades of the 20th century, until it was struck by the crippling blow of the Great Depression in 1929, which virtually wiped out the demand for precious stones overseas. This devastated the local pearling economy, while the discovery of a reliable method of producing cultured pearls soon afterwards wiped out what was left of the industry, which had provided a livelihood for much of the population. Poverty became increasingly widespread, and the Deira side of the Creek revolted against Maktoum rule, leading to a state of virtual civil war within the city.

Fortunately, a man for the moment was at hand, in the form of the redoubtable Sheikh Rashid, one of Dubai's most visionary leaders. Rashid didn't officially become ruler until the death of his father Sheikh Saeed in 1958, but served as de facto leader for many years before his formal accession. His first major act was to crush the Deira rebellion in 1939, after which he had to face down a further wave of popular protests inspired by the democratic Arab Nationalist movement led by Egyptian president Gamal Nasser.

Life on Dubai's Creek before bridges transformed the area

It wasn't until the end of the 1950s that Rashid was able to realise his vision for the city. His first act was to dredge the Creek. This he did, somehow raising the funds for what was then, in terms of Dubai's wealth, an enormously expensive project. Dredging finished by 1961, establishing Dubai as the best-equipped port in the region. Further projects followed in rapid succession: Dubai's first airport (which opened in 1960), the first bridge across the Creek (the Maktoum Bridge, erected in 1963) and, most importantly, the huge new Port Rashid (which opened in 1971), which did more than anything else to drive modern Dubai's nascent economy. At the same time, as if to prove that fortune favours the brave, oil was discovered. Reserves were relatively modest compared to those found in neighbouring Abu Dhabi, but the subsequent revenues provided much of the money needed to fund Dubai's major new infrastructure projects and launch it into the modern industrial world.

INDEPENDENCE

In the same year that Port Rashid opened, Dubai became independent. The various 'Trucial States', as they had previously been known, had been living comfortably under British protection since 1820 and had no particular wish to see the end of Britain's military presence in the Gulf. Forced to look elsewhere for protection, the emirates of Dubai, Abu Dhabi, Sharjah, Ajman, Fujairah and Umm al Qaiwain formed a new confederation known as the United Arab Emirates (a seventh emirate, Ras al Khaimah, joined soon afterwards), to be led by the ruler of Abu Dhabi, with the ruler of Dubai as his second-in-command. Many observers feared the new country would rapidly fall apart (or, alternatively, fall prey to a larger and more powerful neighbour), although more than 40 years later it is still going strong, and has proved more of a success than perhaps anyone could have hoped for at the time.

Dubai, meanwhile, continued to prosper within the new UAE. Business was booming, the population was growing steadily, and further landmarks appeared at the behest of the indefatigable

⊘ NAMING RIGHTS

As Dubai teetered on the edge of bankruptcy in 2008, rumour abounded as to what price the rulers of Abu Dhabi would extract in return for bailing out their profligate neighbour. In the end, Dubai wasn't obliged to relinquish any of its commercial crown jewels in return for the loan, although it did make one small but richly symbolic concession, renaming the vast new Burj Dubai skyscraper as the Burj Khalifa in honour of Abu Dhabi's ruler Sheikh Khalifa bin Zayed Al Nahyan – meaning that the name of a rival ruler now adorns the loftiest and most visible building in the city.

Sheikh Rashid, including the new World Trade Centre, Jebel Ali Port, the Shindagha Tunnel and the city's dry docks.

SHEIKH MOHAMMED

Sheikh Rashid suffered a stroke in 1982, and although he survived until 1990, the day-to-day running of the city increasingly fell to his four sons. Of these, the eldest, Sheikh Maktoum, was appointed official heir to the throne, although it was

Sheikh Mohammed, Vice President and Prime Minister of the UAE, as well as emir of Dubai

increasingly Rashid's third son, Mohammed, who provided the imagination and impetus that drove development. Mohammed continued to tread in his father's entrepreneurial footsteps, although focusing increasingly on service industries rather than infrastructure projects. His first major coup was the founding in 1985 of Emirates, now one of the world's most successful airlines. He also oversaw the creation of numerous free-trade zones and specialised business enclaves, most notably Dubai Media City and Dubai Internet City, backed with business-friendly legislation, which encouraged large numbers of blue-chip global companies to set up their regional headquarters here.

Realizing, too, that Dubai lacked global presence and an iconic landmark by which it could be recognized, Sheikh Mohammed decided to build one – the magical Burj Al Arab, whose hugely distinctive sail-shaped outline has made the city familiar to millions. Further spectacular mega-developments followed,

Political reality

The UAE is not just glitz and glamour. Beneath its alluring façade, there is the harsh reality of an authoritative state. According to Amnesty International, the country has mounted an unprecedented crackdown on dissent since 2011, when a group of activists called for political reforms, including an elected parliament.

including the world's largest artificial island (Palm Jumeirah), its biggest shopping centre (Dubai Mall), its biggest fountain (Dubai Fountain), its tallest hotel, JW Marriott Marquis, and, most strikingly, the world's tallest building, the monumental Burj Khalifa.

LOOKING AHEAD

Then, in 2008, just as it seemed the boom would never end, Dubai was brought crashing down to earth as the result of the global credit crunch. The real-estate market collapsed, investment fled, and Dubai, which had been announcing the launch of record-breaking developments on an almost daily basis, found itself suddenly teetering on the edge of bankruptcy. Abu Dhabi came to the rescue with a massive bail-out package, although many of the city's megaprojects were cancelled or put on indefinite hold (see page 12).

Still, the city is facing the future with optimism. Its attractiveness has been steadily growing in recent years, and Dubai International Airport overtook Heathrow as the world's busiest international airport in 2015. Passenger traffic will likely hit new record highs as Dubai gears up for its stint as the World Expo city in 2020, the first time the event is to be held in the Middle East. With the theme 'Connecting Minds, Creating the Future', the 438-hectare purpose-built expo site will be another jaw-dropping project. The exhibition will run well into 2021, when the UAE will celebrate its 50th anniversary.

HISTORICAL LANDMARKS

2700–2000BC A Bronze Age settlement is established at Al Sufouh.

1st century BC An Iron Age village is established at Al Ghusais.

6th century AD The Sassanids set up a trading post in Jumeira.

AD632 The region converts to Islam. Arabic replaces Aramaic.

1580 Earliest surviving reference to 'Dibei' by Gasparo Balbi of Venice.

1793 A dependency of Abu Dhabi, Dubai is a fishing and pearling village of 1,200 people located around the Creek.

1833 Maktoum Bin Buti Al Maktoum and 800 members of the Al Bu Falasah section of the Bani Yas tribe settle in Shindagha.

1853 The Perpetual Treaty of Maritime Truce is signed by Britain and local sheikhs. The region becomes the Trucial Coast.

1902 Increased customs duties in the Persian port of Lingah prompt more foreign traders to migrate to Dubai's free-trade zone.

1912 Sheikh Saeed Bin Maktoum becomes ruler.

1958 Sheikh Rashid Bin Saeed, 'the Father of Dubai', becomes ruler.

1966 Oil is discovered in Dubai's offshore Fatah field.

1969 Oil production begins.

1971 The UAE becomes an independent federation on 2 December. Abu Dhabi's Sheikh Zayed Bin Sultan Al Nahyan becomes president, Sheikh Rashid of Dubai is appointed vice-president.

1980s First mall (Al Ghurair Centre, 1981), Dubai Duty Free (1983), Emirates airline (1985) and Jebel Ali Free Zone (1985) established.

1990 Sheikh Maktoum Bin Rashid becomes ruler.

2006 Sheikh Maktoum dies. Sheikh Mohammed becomes ruler of Dubai.

2008 The world financial crisis hits Dubai.

2010 Opening of the Burj Khalifa, the world's tallest building.

2013 Population of Dubai reaches 2.1 million, up from 59,000 in 1967.

2014 Amnesty International reproaches UAE for an unparalleled clampdown on dissent since 2011, when a group of activists called for political reforms.

2015 UAE takes part in the Saudi Arabian airstrikes on the Houthis in Yemen.

2017 Five UAE diplomats are killed in bombings in Afghanistan. UAE are accused of hacking Qatari government media sites.

The Burj Khalifa dominates the city

WHERE TO GO

Dubai – pronounced 'do buy', not 'dew buy' – is an extraordinary and surprising city. The cosmopolitan home to the vast majority of the Emirate's 3.1 million strong population, its climate and beaches have met the two traditional holiday requirements of sun and sand for decades. Indeed, at one time sun and sand were about all the city could offer, apart from the Arabian souks on Dubai Creek.

But in the last two decades, that has changed dramatically. The government's drive to uncover, preserve or rebuild heritage sites, which was initiated in the mid-1980s and gathered pace in the '90s, along with the development of a fascinating skyline with camera-pleasing landmarks such as Emirates Towers and the sail-shaped Burj Al Arab hotel, the development of world-class shopping malls and the promotion of the emirate's desert interior as a 'safari' destination for rough and ready exploration or luxury, reserve-based retreats means there are now so many places of interest that visitors can find themselves with little time for the beach.

Within the lifetime of its oldest residents, Dubai has grown from three settlements of palm-frond, mud-brick and coral-stone dwellings based around the mouth of its 15km- (9 mile-) long creek – Shindagha, Bur Dubai and Deira, each little changed from the century before – to a modern metropolis that incorporates the once-distant fishing village of Jumeirah and sprawls as far west as Jebel Ali Port, some 30km (19 miles) along the coast.

In the 1990s, the growth corridor was along Sheikh Zayed Road, southwest of the creek. Today, this eight-lane highway to Abu Dhabi boasts a number of eye-catching skyscrapers, including the world's tallest building – the Burj Khalifa (www.burjkhalifa.

Bur Dubai and Deira

Relations between the two Creekside districts of Bur Dubai and Deira have not always been harmonious. During the late 1930s, Deira rebelled against the authority of the Bur Dubai-based Sheikh Saeed, declaring independence. Order was only restored when Saeed's son, the young Sheikh Rashid, arrived in Deira with his Bedu retainers and shot down the rebel leaders. Those who survived were blinded in one eye as punishment and only allowed to keep their remaining eye on payment of a sizeable sum.

ae) – and, further west, the spectacular massed high-rises of the Dubai Marina development. More recently, Dubai has been extensively expanding into the sea and the desert.

But even as Dubai undergoes dramatic expansion to gear up for the millions more foreign residents, business travellers and tourists it hopes to attract in the years ahead, Dubai Creek remains the established heart and soul of the city. Dubai began on the banks of the Creek, and for visitors there is no better place to begin discovering the city.

SHINDAGHA

The historic **Shindagha** peninsula on the western bank of Dubai's tidal Creek has now been swallowed by Bur Dubai, but was once a distinct settlement, separated by an arm of the Creek, known as Ghubaiba, which flooded at high tide.

A curling promontory at the mouth of the Creek, Shindagha is the most likely site of the original fishing and pearling village, which would have consisted of simple palm-frond dwellings called *barasti* or *arish*, and perhaps a few mud-brick houses. The main residential area for Dubai's Arab population in the 1800s and early 1900s, Shindagha was the traditional seat of the community's leaders. It was here in 1823 that Mohammed Bin Hazza welcomed the Persia-based British Political Resident in the Gulf, Lieutenant J. McLeod. Through an interpreter, McLeod briefed Hazza on British intentions along the coast, including plans to place a representative agent in the then more established settlement of Sharjah, to the north.

It was here, too, that 800 members of the Al Bu Falasah subsection of the Bani Yas tribe settled after seceding from Abu Dhabi in 1833. Led by Sheikh Maktoum Bin Buti and Sheikh Obaid Bin Saeed Bin Rashid, the Bani Yas influx transformed the politics of a community that had numbered around 1,200 people before their arrival. Maktoum became its new ruler, establishing the Al Maktoum dynasty that rules Dubai to this day.

Shindagha waterfront, on the western bank of the Creek

HERITAGE MUSEUMS

The Maktoum family's former home, built in 1896 for Sheikh Maktoum Bin Hasher Al Maktoum but now named after his successor Sheikh Saeed, who ruled the emirate from 1912 to 1958, was rebuilt in the 1980s and is a museum of early life in Dubai. The imposing **Sheikh Saeed al Maktoum House** ❶ (Sat–Thu 8am–8.30pm, Fri 3–10pm) contains photographs, an exhibition about fishing and pearling, coins, stamps and historic documents. Located on a quiet stretch of the Creekside promenade, a 10-minute walk from the bustle of the Bur Dubai *abra* (water taxi) station, the two-storey structure, built of coral stone and covered

---

◑ BREEDING FALCONS

The fastest creature on the planet has been trained for hunting purposes for thousands of years, but in the 21st century the ancient skill of falconry is maintained for sport rather than survival. Before weapons, peregrine falcons – which can achieve speeds of 320kph (200mph) in a dive – were used by *bedu* hunters to catch food. Wild falcons were caught and trained in two or three weeks at the start of the hunting season in October. Favoured prey was the houbara bustard, a desert bird the size of a heron, whose meat could be vital to a family's survival. At the end of the season, in March, the falcon would be freed.

Today, falcons are no longer captured, but reared from hatchlings. Even so, they require human contact on a daily basis, or else they become wild and unreliable. Especially keen falconers fly to Pakistan for hunting expeditions, their falcons travelling on their own special passports. Falcons are also put to practical use: Dubai's Burj Al Arab hotel employs a falconer to keep pigeons – and pigeon droppings – off the landmark property.

in lime and sand-coloured plaster, is a fine example of late-19th-century Emirati architecture, with Persian influences. Architectural features include arched doorways, sculpted window overhangs, vaulted high-beamed ceilings and carved trellis screens, but the overriding feature of the house is its four *barjeel*, or wind-towers, an innovative early form of air conditioning introduced by traders from Iran. The second-floor

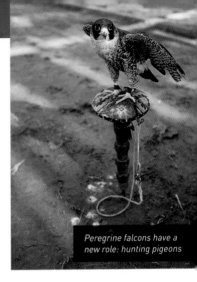

Peregrine falcons have a new role: hunting pigeons

bedrooms and balconies above the high perimeter walls offered vantage points for Sheikh Saeed, grandfather of the present ruler, and his son Sheikh Rashid, 'the Father of Dubai', to watch the sea trade moving in and out of the Creek.

Today the view out to sea, across the busy road that leads to Shindagha Tunnel, is dominated by **Port Rashid**. Construction on this deep-water harbour began in 1967, instigated by Sheikh Rashid during an era of massive public works funded by the emirate's new oil revenues and designed to provide it with a diversified modern industrial and commercial base. The 3,300 sq m (35,522 sq ft) **Dubai Cruise Terminal** at Port Rashid makes the Shindagha peninsula a convenient first stop for cruise-ship passengers.

Port Rashid aside, Shindagha, which consisted of 250 homes at the turn of the 20th century, was neglected in the rush to develop the city in the early years of the oil boom. When Sheikh Saeed died in 1958, the Maktoums moved away. But the regeneration of this stretch of the Creek, which followed the rebuilding of Sheikh Saeed's house, has seen the reconstruction of a string of other heritage houses. These include the Sheikh Juma al Maktoum House, an attractive traditional building from 1928, which now houses the interesting **Traditional Architecture Museum** (Sun–Thu 8.30am–8.30pm, Fri 2.30-8.30pm), with informative displays on architecture and

☉ PEARL DIVING

Before 'black gold' there were pearls. In the centuries before oil was discovered, pearling was the mainstay of the Dubai economy, involving the majority of the Creek settlements' men and boys. From June to September, boats of between 15 and 60 men stayed at sea for up to four months, moving from one pearl oyster bed to another and sheltering from storms on Gulf islets. Equipped with little more than a nose clip, ear plugs and finger pads, and surviving on a diet of fish and rationed water, the men would dive on weighted ropes to depths of around 15m (49ft) up to 50 times a day. In two or three minutes under water they could collect up to a dozen pearl oysters.

Pearls were graded according to their size, colour and shape. In the early 20th century, the best pearls or *jiwan* (a derivative of 'Grade One' or 'G-One') could fetch 1,500 rupees, but while Dubai's pearl merchants grew wealthy, a diver's wages for the entire season could be as little as 30–60 rupees. Famous for their rose colouring, Dubai pearls were traded in India, from where they were sent to Paris. The popularity of the Japanese cultured pearl from the 1930s devastated the Gulf industry virtually overnight. After struggling on for another decade, the last great pearling expedition sailed from Dubai in 1949.

building in Dubai and the Emirates, and the nearby **Sheikh Obaid Bin Thani House**, dating from 1916.

A short walk north along the waterside lies the **Heritage Village ❷** (Sun-Thu 8am–8pm, Fri 3–10pm), which serves as a focus for cultural activities, music and dance on public holidays and during the annual Dubai Shopping Festival in January (although the 'village' can be very quiet at other times), offering a

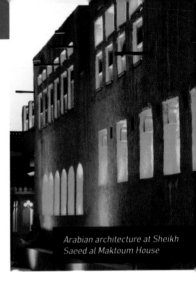

Arabian architecture at Sheikh Saeed al Maktoum House

glimpse of what life was like in the Emirates in the days before oil. On display within the compound are the camel- and goat-hair tents that nomadic *bedu* used before they settled on the coast, and houses of mud and stone that were typical of Dubai's mountain region around the inland enclave of Hatta. The nearby **Diving Village** (currently closed for renovation) presents a nautical variation on the heritage theme, with demonstrations and displays about pearl diving and the manufacture of fishing nets and traditional boats, which were made of palm fronds and wood.

SHINDAGHA PROMENADE

One of the most attractive features of Shindagha, however, is the view from its promenade back along the creek, past the busy *abra* stations, the waterfront at Dubai Old Souk, the Juma Grand Mosque with its impressive 70-m- (231-ft-) high minaret and the Emiri Diwan (or Ruler's Court), towards architect

Carlos Ott's sail-shaped National Bank of Dubai building and the triangular blue wedge that is the Dubai Chamber of Commerce. With the buildings crowded in on either side of the waterway, the *abras* packed with passengers criss-crossing the creek and the occasional passing *dhow* loaded with exports for Pakistan, India or East Africa, the scene is reminiscent of a Canaletto painting, recalling an old nickname for Dubai you don't often hear these days – 'Venice of the Middle East'.

BUR DUBAI

If Shindagha was the residential district of old Dubai, with no shops or souks, then **Bur Dubai** was its central business district. It was here that the first purpose-built office building, Bait Al Wakeel, was constructed in the early 1930s to house British agents and trade missions. Here, too, stood the headquarters of the British Bank of the Middle East, the city's first bank, established in 1946.

Historically more cosmopolitan than Shindagha, Bur Dubai was home to Persian and Indian merchants who settled here with their families from 1894, when Sheikh Maktoum Bin Hasher declared free-trade status for the city, though the major influx of immigrants came after 1902, when customs duties at Lingah, on the Persian coast, were increased and Bur Dubai became a more attractive hub for trade. The Persian influence on the architecture of Bur Dubai is still evident, in the 25 surviving wind-tower houses that make up the Al Fahidi Historical Neighbourhood.

DUBAI MUSEUM

The oldest surviving structure in Bur Dubai is **Al Fahidi Fort**, which was built between 1787 and 1799 to guard the landward approach to the town. The Portuguese-influenced fortress served as the ruler's residence and the seat of government in the past, and would have been a refuge for the inhabitants of the coastal community in the event of attack. The building itself – a simple, square, high-walled compound with corner towers covered in sun-baked plaster – is an arresting sight among the modern apartment blocks and office buildings of Al Fahidi Street. A stunning wooden pearling *dhow* stands on the plaza beside it.

Since 1971, the fort has housed the **Dubai Museum ❸** (Sat–Thu 8.30am–8.30pm, Fri 2–8.30pm). Most of the excellent exhibits are displayed in underground galleries, including a multi-media overview of the development of Dubai, as well as detailed dioramas recreating scenes from everyday life in the years before oil. Among the artefacts displayed here are finds from the archaeological sites at Al Qusais and Jumeirah, dating from the Iron Age and 6th century respectively.

Between the fort and the Creek is the landmark **Juma Grand Mosque** (entry to Muslims only), one of the oldest in Dubai, which has the tallest minaret in the city, nine large domes, 45 small domes and space for 1,200 worshippers. It was built in 1900 and rebuilt in 1998.

AL FAHIDI HISTORICAL NEIGHBOURHOOD

As recently as the mid-1990s, **Al Fahidi Historical Neighbourhood** (Bastakiya) ❹ was a run-down place with up to 100 people often crammed into a single house. Now, thanks to a restoration programme undertaken by Dubai Municipality's Historical Buildings Section, it has become a case study for urban conservation in the Arab world and is enjoying a new lease of life as the city's arts quarter – particularly vibrant during the annual SIKKA Art Fair in March.

Located on the Creekside next to the Emiri Diwan, or Ruler's Palace, Bastakiya would not have been built were it not for the city's open-door policy to foreign trade. Its original residents were wealthy traders from Bastak and Lingah on the coast of modern-day Iran – hence the name. They settled here, close to their shops in the nearby Bur Dubai Souk, between 1902 and 1950, the period in which their distinctive wind-tower homes were built.

The quarter's famous wind-towers, which can rise to a height of 15m (49ft), were an early form of air conditioning – the open sides of each square tower caught the breeze and channelled it into rooms below. The walls of each house were made of coral stone, which, thanks to its porous nature, has low thermal conductivity, keeping temperatures inside to a minimum. For privacy and security, there were no windows on the ground floor, just a few ventilation holes, which gives the narrow alleyways between the brown, plaster-covered buildings an *Arabian Nights-type* atmosphere.

The old merchant quarter of Bastakiya

Wonderfully restored examples of Al Fahidi's historic houses include the venerable **Majlis Gallery** (www.themajlisgallery.com; Sun–Thu 10am–6pm, Sat 9am–5pm), which was founded by British expatriate Alison Collins in her family home in 1989; the **XVA Gallery** (www.xvagallery.com; daily 10am–6pm), which has a calming courtyard coffee shop; and **Bastakiah Nights** (tel: 04 353 7772; daily 6.30–10.30am, 12.30–3pm and 6.30pm–12am), an Arabian–Iranian restaurant in one of the quarter's oldest and largest houses, built in three phases between 1890 and 1940.

Al Fahidi Historical Neighbourhood is also home to the **Sheikh Mohammed Centre For Cultural Understanding** (tel: 04 353 6666; www.cultures.ae; Sun–Thu 9am–5pm, Sat 9am–1pm), which organises walking tours of the district, as well as guided tours of **Jumeirah Mosque** (Sat 9am, Sun, Tue and Thu 10.30am) and visits to local homes, to increase awareness and understanding between cultures. A stroll around the neighbourhood will throw up other cultural curios, such as the **Arabic Calligraphy Museum** and a **Stamp Museum**, and photo-opportunities abound in its alleyways and plazas.

BUR DUBAI SOUK

Known variously as the Abra Souk, Grand Souk Bur Dubai and the Textile Souk, **Bur Dubai Souk ❺** (most shops open Sat–Thu 10am–1pm and 4–10pm, Fri 4–10pm) runs parallel to the creek below Al Fahidi Fort. Among its textile shops and stalls is a forerunner of the gleaming skyscrapers on Sheikh Zayed Road – **Bait al Wakeel**, the city's first office building. Commissioned by Sheikh Saeed in 1930 and completed soon afterwards, it was previously known as the Gray Mackenzie Building after the British company based there, licensed shipping agents in Dubai since 1891. Restored in 1995, Bait Al Wakeel is now a pleasant waterfront restaurant.

Nearby, at the water's edge, **Bur Dubai Old Souk Abra Station** is a fascinating spot to stand and watch the traffic on the Creek. For one dirham you can catch an *abra* (water taxi) from here to the Al Sabkha Abra Station on the Deira side of the Creek. From the water, you will get an excellent view of the traditional buildings on the Creek front. However, if you want to cross to the gold or spice souks in Deira, walk on to **Bur Dubai Abra Station**, near the entrance to Bur Dubai Souk – the *abras* that depart from here will drop you closer to the souks. Air-conditioned water-buses also operate from both stations.

For more contemporary shopping, **Al Fahidi Road** is lined with shop windows stacked high with shiny watches, mobile phones and other electronics, as well as

Airline tower

There is a plan afoot to transform six Dubai metro stations into art galleries, showcasing Islamic art and Arabic calligraphy.

An array of colourful textiles at a Dubai souk

colourful textile shops offering a wide variety of silks and fabrics from India. Further inland, Bur Dubai's main thoroughfare, **Khalid Bin al Waleed Road**, has the city's largest concentration of computer shops, while at its junction with Sheikh Khalifa Bin Zayed Road (Trade Centre Road) stands the expansive **BurJuman** (www. burjuman.com; shops: Sat–Wed 10am–10pm, Thu–Fri 10am–11pm, supermarket: daily 9am–midnight, restaurants: Sat–Wed 10am–11pm, Thu–Fri 10am–midnight), the largest and most upmarket mall in the old city and also the departure point for the amphibious **Wonder Bus** (tel: 04 359 5656; www.wonderbustours. net), one of Dubai's most unusual sightseeing vehicles.

AL SEEF ROAD

Away from the heritage sights and the shops, **Al Seef Road**, at the Creek end of Sheikh Khalifa Bin Zayed Road, is popular with fishermen, walkers and joggers. Day or night, the view from

A fabric salesman in Deira

the quayside in front of the British Embassy compound across the water to Carlos Ott's 125m (410ft) **National Bank of Dubai Building ⑥** is one of the best in the city. In daylight, in particular, the bank's convex, sail-shaped glass facade reflects activity on the Creek below it, while towards dusk, when the sun hits the glass panels at just the right angle, the building shoots off dazzling rays of light. Next to it stands the triangular blue Dubai Chamber of Commerce. Water taxis and air-conditioned Waterbuses operate out of **Al Seef Abra Station**.

DEIRA

One of the three settlements that comprised early Dubai, Deira lies across the Creek from Shindagha and Bur Dubai. After settling in Shindagha in 1833, the Maktoums had to wait until 1841 before their power base extended to Deira. That same year, an outbreak of smallpox on the west side of the Creek prompted many of its inhabitants to cross to Deira and settle here. The early dwellings were made of palm fronds, but after fire ravaged the community in 1894, more substantial homes were constructed, using coral stone and gypsum.

Deira's great souk, Al Souk al Kabeer, was built in 1850. Stocked with imported goods, offloaded from *dhows* on the nearby Creek, it was the largest market in the region in the second half of the 19th century. By 1908, according to the historian and geographer G.G. Lorimer, there were 1,600 houses and 350 shops in Deira, compared to 200 houses and 50 shops in Bur Dubai.

Together with Bur Dubai, Deira formed the commercial heart of Dubai, but it was also the district where new services emerged: the children of Shindagha and Bur Dubai crossed to Deira for an education after the city's first school was established here in 1912, and people came to Deira for medical treatment after the first hospital on the Trucial Coast, Al Maktoum Hospital, was established here in 1949.

THE GOLD SOUK

Arguably the most famous attraction in Deira today is the **Gold Souk** ❼ (most shops open Sat–Thu 10am–1pm and 4–10pm, Fri 4–10pm), a cluster of streets shaded by a high roof in the Al Ras neighbourhood.

One of the largest centres in the world for gold bullion, Dubai was trading in gold long before 'black gold' was discovered. In fact, when the bottom fell out of the local pearl market in the 1930s, after the development of the cultured pearl in Japan, it was gold that saw Dubai through one of its leanest periods. Historically, it was demand from India that drove trade, and even today, it is the softer, higher-carat golds favoured on the subcontinent that predominate in the souk's window displays.

With 700 shops, Dubai Gold Souk is claimed to be the biggest in the world, and with the lowest prices, too (haggling is expected), offering a huge range of intricately worked necklaces, bangles, rings, earrings and brooches in 14-, 18-, 22- and 24-carat gold.

A magnet for visitors throughout the year, the souk is particularly busy during the month-long Dubai Shopping Festival in January (www.visitdubaishoppingfestival.com), when the area becomes a focal point for the raffle draws and street entertainment that are features of the festival. The biggest draw, however, are the discounts offered by traders throughout the month.

THE SPICE SOUK

Closer to the Creek, at the intersection of Old Baladiya Street and the Creekside Bani Yas Road, is Dubai's **Spice Souk** ❽ (most shops open Sat–Thu 10am–1pm and 4–10pm, Fri 4–10pm). Fronted by the restored heritage buildings of Deira Old Souk, just across the road from the Deira Old Souk Abra Station, the Spice Souk is smaller than it once was, but what it lacks in quantity it makes up for in atmosphere: the lanes here are much narrower and darker than the streets of the Gold Souk and the air is scented by the colourful offerings displayed outside each shop: cloves, cardamom, cinnamon, saffron, rose petals and incense. At an undefined point, the Spice Souk becomes **Deira Old Souk**, which offers an uninspiring selection of cheap cooking utensils.

AL AHMADIYA SCHOOL

There are several well-preserved historic sites in Deira close to the Gold Souk. Foremost among them is **Al Ahmadiya School** ❾ (Sat–Thu 8am–7.30pm, Fri 2.30–7.30pm), which is located on Al Ahmadiya Street in the Al Ras area, a short walk west of the Gold Souk. Al Ahmadiya School was the first semi-formal school in Dubai when it was established in 1912, and one of the Emirate's first regular schools when formal education was introduced in 1956.

Before it was founded by local pearl merchant Ahmad Bin Dalmouk, after whom it was named, boys were taught the Koran, Arabic calligraphy and arithmetic in their own homes by a man or woman known as *Al Muttawa* – literally 'volunteer'. With the establishment of semi-formal schools along the Trucial Coast,

Spices, nuts and seeds on sale at the Spice Souk

typically financed by pearl merchants, the curriculum expanded to include mathematics, sciences, history, literature and astronomy.

Built in three phases, Al Ahmadiya School was initially a single-storey structure with 11 classrooms and a *liwan* (veranda), around an inner courtyard. The upper floor was added in 1920. In 1932, following the collapse of the pearl trade, and with it the local economy, the school was forced to close, but it reopened in 1937 with a government subsidy. In the 1950s, with the introduction of a formal education system, English, sociology and more science subjects were added to the curriculum and student numbers increased. By 1962, the school had 823 students – more than it could comfortably accommodate. In 1963, when it moved to a new, larger site, the original building was closed.

During its restoration by Dubai Municipality's Historical Buildings Section, authentic building materials such as coral stone, gypsum and sandalwood were used to recreate Al

Al Ahmadiya School, Dubai's first, is now a museum of education

Ahmadiya School as its famous old boys would have known it. Among its illustrious alumni are Sheikh Rashid Bin Saeed Al Maktoum, ruler of Dubai between 1958 and 1990, and his third son Sheikh Mohammed Bin Rashid Al Maktoum, the current ruler of Dubai and UAE vice-president and prime minister. The school opened as a museum of education in 2000.

HERITAGE HOUSE

Next to Al Ahmadiya School is the similarly time-warped **Heritage House** (Sat–Thu 8am–7.30pm, Fri 8am–2.30pm), which was also restored in the mid-1990s and opened to the public in 2000. The former residence of the Bin Dalmouk family, the pearl traders who established the school, the oldest part of Heritage House dates back to 1890, when it was built for Mohammed Bin Saeed Bin Muzaina. Sheikh Ahmad Bin Dalmouk expanded the house when he assumed ownership in 1910.

Today, the house is preserved as it would have been in the 1950s, offering an intriguing snapshot of the social life of Dubai's wealthier inhabitants during that period. Notable features include the separate men's and women's *majlis* (meeting rooms), where guests would sit on embroidered silk or wool pillows around the edge of a Persian-carpeted floor, drinking Arabian coffee and discussing the economic, social and political issues of the day.

Opposite Heritage House and Al Ahmadiya School, the small, single-storey building constructed in a similar style is Bin Lootah Mosque, built in 1910. Restored in 1995, the mosque is still used for prayers and is not open to the public.

EAST OF THE GOLD SOUK

Exiting the Gold Souk via the main entrance and heading east along Sikkat al Khail Road brings you immediately to the so-called **Perfume Souk,** comprising a line of shops along Sikkat al Khail and Al Soor streets which sell a mix of Western brands (not necessarily genuine) and more flowery local scents. Many places can also mix up a bespoke perfume for you from the rows of glass scent bottles lined up behind the counters.

Continue up Al Soor Street and cross the pedestrian footbridge over the main road to reach one of the most interesting markets in the city, **Deira Fish, Meat and Vegetable Market** ⓾ (5am–1pm, 5–11pm), located between Al Khaleej Road and the Gulf. Although it is open throughout the day, the best time to visit is early in the morning when the market is busy with porters pushing wheelbarrows full of seafood between the refrigerated lorries and market halls. The variety of species is fascinating, some recognisable,

Flying boat days

Dubai Creek was a landing area for Imperial Airways' flying boats in the late 1930s and 1940s.

some not, but including shark, barracuda, tuna, kingfish, sea bream, red snapper, hammour (Gulf cod), mackerel, sardines, squid and king prawns.

Returning to the Perfume Souk and continuing along Sikkat al Khail Road on your right, you'll see the narrow alleyways of the **Deira Covered Souk** which straggles all the way down into Al Sabkha neighbourhood, with hundreds of shoebox shops selling a fairly humdrum array of workaday household items.

MUNICIPALITY MUSEUM

The modern home of Dubai Municipality is on the Creekside next to the Radisson SAS Hotel, but its former headquarters has been preserved as another of Deira's heritage buildings. Located on the edge of the Spice Souk, across Bani Yas Road from the Deira Old Souk Abra Station, the **Municipality Museum** (Sun–Thu 8am–2pm) is a simple but elegant two-storey structure with a long wooden balcony. Restored in 1999, the museum now hosts assorted civic documents and old photographs.

DEIRA CREEKSIDE

The Deira side of the Creek is much busier than the Bur Dubai waterfront, thanks to the *dhow* **wharves** ⓫ that line it between the Deira Old Souk and Al Sabkha abra stations. Although Dubai has two modern container ports at Port Rashid and Jebel Ali, as well as a busy international airport, traditional wooden dhows are still used for transporting varied cargoes between Dubai and its historic trading partners in India, Pakistan and East Africa.

The activity on and around the *dhows*, which are sometimes moored three or four abreast, the tyres, automotive spare parts and electrical goods stacked high on the quayside without fear of theft, the weather-beaten features of the old sailors and the timeless design of the vessels themselves make a wander along Deira's busy quays a high-light of any visit to Dubai.

Continue inland along the Creek for slightly over 1km to reach a second set of *dhow* wharves, occupying a purpose-built pair of quays between the triangular blue Dubai Chamber of Commerce Building and Maktoum Bridge. The quays jut into the creek here, offering an interesting perspective on Carlos Ott's **National Bank of Dubai** building.

Inland from the wharves, it is a short walk to the stylish **Hilton Dubai Creek** and, beyond, to one of Dubai's oldest landmarks, **Clocktower Roundabout**, where the Maktoum Bridge traffic intersects with Al Maktoum Road. Built in 1962, the venerable clocktower features in numerous old photographs. Originally sur-rounded by desert, it is one of the few structures to have survived

Old dhows lining Deira Creekside

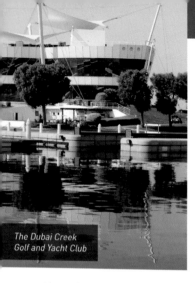

The Dubai Creek Golf and Yacht Club

five decades of development – a rare visual reference point in the changing face of the city. Overlooking Clocktower Roundabout, the identical towers of the **Marriott Executive Apartments Complex** are connected by a sky-bridge that, at 74m (242ft), is the longest in the world.

Not on the Creek, but just a short detour along Al Maktoum Road from Clocktower Roundabout, towards Dubai International Airport, is the **Nasser Bin Abdullatif al Serkal Building**, which is easily distinguished by its Indian-style architecture.

GARHOUD AND BEYOND

Further down Baniyas Road you enter the suburb of **Garhoud**, close to the international airport, and boasting a mixed range of attractions. First up is **Deira City Centre** (www.citycentre deira.com; mall: Sun–Wed 10am–10pm, Thu–Sat 10am–midnight, supermarket: daily 9am–midnight, Thu–Fri until 1am), one of Dubai's oldest mega-malls. It has long since been eclipsed by newer and more glamorous malls across the city, but continues to pull in a loyal crowd of locals, thanks to its wide selection of low-cost shopping outlets, which are busy at any time of the day or night.

Past here stretch the beautifully manicured grounds of the **Dubai Creek Golf Club** (DCGC, www.dubaigolf.com), home to the idyllic **Park Hyatt** hotel, the Dubai Yacht Club (where you'll find a number of lively restaurants, including the excellent The Boardwalk) and the landmark **DCGC clubhouse** ⑫ with its distinctive tapering outline inspired by the shape of the traditional *dhow* sail, with three 'sails' entwined to create a tent-like structure – like a miniature Dubai remake of the Sydney Opera House.

The largest public park on the Deira side of the Creek, **Al Mamzar Beach Park** (Sun–Wed 8am–10pm, Thu–Sat and public holidays until 11pm, Mon and Wed women and children only) is near Dubai's boundary with the neighbouring Emirate of Sharjah. The park, which is on a kilometre-long spit dividing the Gulf from three large lagoons, has four beaches, two swimming pools, lots of greenery, barbecue and picnic areas, children's play areas and an amphitheatre in which international children's productions are performed during the Dubai Shopping Festival.

UMM HURAIR

Moving away from the historic centre of Dubai, there is also plenty to see and do in the districts located to the south and west of Dubai Creek. Although they are referred to locally as 'the Bur Dubai side of the Creek', strictly speaking neighbourhoods such as Umm Hurair and Karama are not actually in Bur Dubai.

CREEKSIDE PARK

Umm Hurair's main attraction is **Creekside Park** ⑬ (Sun–Wed 8am–10pm, Thu–Sat 8am–11pm), which fronts Dubai Creek for over 3km (2 miles) between the

Arabian boats

The name given to wooden boats in the Arabian Gulf is *dhow*, from the Swahili word for boat, *dau*. These traditional cargo and fishing vessels are still a common sight on Dubai Creek.

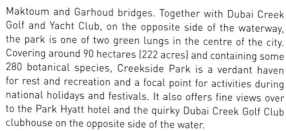

Maktoum and Garhoud bridges. Together with Dubai Creek Golf and Yacht Club, on the opposite side of the waterway, the park is one of two green lungs in the centre of the city. Covering around 90 hectares (222 acres) and containing some 280 botanical species, Creekside Park is a verdant haven for rest and recreation and a focal point for activities during national holidays and festivals. It also offers fine views over to the Park Hyatt hotel and the quirky Dubai Creek Golf Club clubhouse on the opposite side of the water.

The park is also home to the vividly coloured buildings housing **Children's City** (www.childrencity.ae; Sun–Thu 9am–7pm, Fri–Sat 2–8pm) near Gate 1, a fun, interactive learning zone and amusement facility for youngsters aged from two to 15. It houses several exhibits based around educational themes, including nature, space exploration, the human body, and local and international culture. There is also a planetarium and a special area for children under five, as well as daily educational workshops throughout the year.

Bordering the southeastern edge of Creekside Park is **Wonderland Theme and Water Park** (tel: 04 324 3222; www.wonderlanduae.com; currently closed for renovation), a rather old-fashioned funfair and waterpark with around 40 indoor and outdoor rides, including rollercoasters and a log flume, as well as go-karting and paintballing. Its water park component is **Splashland**, which has several waterslides.

WAFI

Not far from Creekside Park is the quirky **Wafi Mall** ⑭ (www.wafi.com; Sat–Wed 10am–10pm, Thu–Fri 10am–midnight), which looks like a little slice of Las Vegas dropped into the middle of the Gulf, with a comic-book, Egyptian-themed design featuring a zany mishmash of huge pharaonic statues, hieroglyphs, spectacular stained-glass windows and half a dozen miniature pyramids dotted across the sprawling rooflines. It is kitsch but entertaining, while the complex also provides one of the city's most attractive shopping and eating destinations.

Beneath the Wafi complex is the beautiful **Khan Murjan Souk** (Sat–Wed 10am–10pm, Thu–Fri 10am–midnight), inspired by the legendary fourteenth-century Khan Murjan Souk in Baghdad and home to over a hundred shops retailing all manner of upmarket Arabian (plus some Indian) handicrafts. This is one of Dubai's finest exercises in Orientalist kitsch, with virtually every available surface covered in lavishly detailed Arabian-style design, featuring elaborate Moroccan-style tilework, intricately carved wooden doors and ceilings, and huge hanging lamps.

The impressive entrance to the Egyptian-themed Wafi Mall

Next door to Wafi – and continuing the Egyptian theme – the vast postmodern pyramid of the **Raffles Hotel** provides the area with its most dramatic landmark, visible for miles around and particularly impressive after dusk, when the glass-walled summit of the pyramid is lit up from within, glowing magically in the darkness. Inside, the main foyer is well worth a look, with huge Egyptian-style columns covered in colourful hieroglyphs.

KARAMA

Some 2km (1 mile) away to the northwest, the low-rent suburb of **Karama** is one of the least exclusive and most popular shopping destinations in Dubai. A nondescript, and in places plain ugly, inner-city neighbourhood of 1970s low-rise apartment buildings packed with ground-floor shops and 'ethnic' eateries,

The Emirates Towers

Karama is Dubai's 'bargain basement', famous for its thriving trade in fake-designer gear and other cheap and cheerful stuff – you won't get more than a few paces into the main **Karama Souk** 🄵 before being regaled with offers of 'cheap copy watch', and the like. The quality of many of the fakes is surprisingly high, although prices can be unexpectedly steep – if you do decide to buy, check workmanship carefully and bargain like mad.

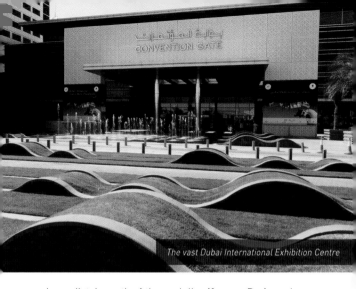

The vast Dubai International Exhibition Centre

Immediately north of the souk lies **Karama Park**, a pleasant square of grass surrounded by dozens of inexpensive but generally excellent curry houses that have earned Karama the nickname 'curry corridor'. This is the social heart of the suburb, usually with half a dozen games of cricket in progress after dark, and crowds of strolling expat Indians, Pakistanis and Filipinos wandering beneath the trees.

Dubai Garden Glow ⑯ in Zabeel Park (south of the souk; www.dubaigardenglow.com; 4pm-midnight) is a must see for both adults and children. The effects of the colourful illuminations are more prominent after sunset.

The most recent addition to the area is the giant **Dubai Frame** ⑰ (www.thedubaiframe.com; daily 10am-7pm). This new Dubai landmark is 93m wide (305ft) and 150m high (492ft) and mimics the shape of a photo frame. The top floor has a glass panel for 360 degree views and the museum on the

The towering skyscrapers of Sheikh Zayed Road

ground floor displays the evolution of Dubai's development from a fishing village to the cosmopolitan city it is today.

SHEIKH ZAYED ROAD AND DOWNTOWN DUBAI

The greatest concentration of landmark buildings in Dubai is on **Sheikh Zayed Road**, between Trade Centre Roundabout and Interchange No. 1. From 1979 to the late 1990s, the most significant structure on this stretch of the highway was the white, 39-storey, 149-m-(489-ft-) high **Dubai World Trade Centre** building (www.dwtc.com), at the northern end of the strip, which features on the country's Dhs100 banknote. Once the tallest building in the Middle East, it has long since been overtaken by much larger and more glamorous structures further down the road, although the adjacent exhibition halls at the **Dubai International Exhibition Centre** still see plenty of visitors during their regular programme of international trade shows and events.

Just south of the Trade Centre rise the iconic **Emirates Towers ⑱**, completed in 2000, which consist of a 355-m- (1,163-ft-) high office tower – at one point the tallest building in the Middle East and Europe – and the 309-m- (1,014-ft-) high Jumeirah Emirates Towers Hotel (www.jumeirah.com). Visitors who aren't staying here or who have no business with the blue-chip companies based in the office tower should head there anyway, for a closer look at Hong Kong architect Hazel Wong's slender triangular towers, clad in silver aluminium with copper and silver reflective glass, described by Wong as 'a *pas de deux* in which the building facades capture the changing light of the desert sun and show off the dramatic integrated illumination at nightfall'. Inside the hotel there is a stunning 30-storey atrium with glass elevators whisking guests to one of the highest restaurants in the Middle East, Italian **Alta Badia** (Sun–Thu noon–3pm and daily 6pm–midnight) on the 50th floor, or the separate **Alta Badia Bar** (daily 4pm–3am) on the 51st floor, both of which offer fabulous views of the coast.

In the ground floor of the complex, the **Emirates Towers Boulevard** is home to a small but exclusive collection of shops, with designer outlets including Cartier, Bulgari and Rivoli, alongside an excellent spread of restaurants and bars, including the ever-popular Noodle House (noon–midnight). Dubai's ruler Sheikh Mohammed and his entourage can occasionally be seen popping down here for lunch from their chambers at the summit of the office tower.

SOUTH ALONG SHEIKH ZAYED ROAD

Immediately south of the Emirates Towers, behind the Sheikh Zayed Road high-rises, stretches Dubai's financial district, the **Dubai International Financial Centre** (DIFC) ❿. Entrance to the complex is via The Gate building, a striking office block designed in the shape of an enormous postmodern archway. Tucked away on the east side of the centre is the so-called **Gate Village**, home to a surprisingly wide (and non-financial) array of attractions, including some good bars, restaurants and shops along with a cluster of upmarket art galleries such as Tabari ArtSpace (Building 3, www.tabariartspace.com) and the Ayyam Gallery (Building 3,

Burj Khalifa

www.ayyamgallery.com).
Local office types flock to
the village's watering holes
after dark – one of the most
popular venues is the funky
Zuma Japanese restaurant
(www.zumarestaurant.com;
lunch Sun–Thu 12–3.30pm,
Sat 12.30–4pm; dinner Sat–
Wed 7pm–midnight, Thu–Fri
until 1am).

North and south of the
Emirates Tower along
Sheikh Zayed Road, the
skyscrapers are lined up
shoulder to shoulder, offer-
ing an eclectic compendium of architectural styles ranging from
the elegantly postmodern to the downright weird. Notable landmarks along the way include (on the Emirates Towers side of the
road) the **Fairmont** hotel, inspired by the shape of a wind-tower
and strikingly illuminated in changing colours after dark; **The
Tower**, covered in blue glass with Islamic styling and a distinctive pointed tip; the pencil-thin **Rose Rayhaan** hotel, at 333m
(108ft) the world's third tallest hotel (surpassed in 2012 by JW
Marriott Marquis Dubai. In 2018 both were surpassed by the
Gevora Hotel, Dubai); and the iconic **Dusit Thani** hotel, whose
distinctive outline – like an upside-down tuning fork – is said
to resemble the traditional Thai greeting of two hands pressed
together. On the opposite side of the highway is the imposing
edifice of the Art Deco-influenced **Shangri-La Hotel**; and the
blue-and-white **Chelsea Tower**, with its distinctive square opening on the top bisected by an enormous vertical needle.

THE BURJ KHALIFA

Just west of Interchange No. 1, the massive **Downtown Dubai** development was opened in 2010 and built at the estimated cost of $20 billion. Rising like an enormous needle out of the heart of the development is the staggering **Burj Khalifa ⑳**, the world's tallest building. Opened in early 2010, the tower, at 828m (2,716ft), obliterated all previous records for the world's tallest man-made structure, smashing the previous record for the world's tallest building (formerly held by Taipei 101 in Taiwan, at 509m, 1,670ft) by a staggering 300m (984ft). The tower has also accumulated a host of other superlatives en route, including the building with the most floors (160), the world's highest and fastest elevators, plus the world's highest mosque (158th floor) and highest swimming pool (76th floor). Much of the tower is occupied by private apartments, while 15 of the lower floors are home to the world's first Armani Hotel (www.armanihotels.com).

⊘ CAFÉ CULTURE

Despite the futuristic architecture and roaring traffic, Sheikh Zayed Road is home to a surprisingly lively café scene, with many places tucked into the base of the soaring towers that line the strip. On the eastern (Emirates Towers) side of the road the chintzy Victoriana-inspired **Shakespeare and Co.** (www.shakespeare-and-co.com; daily 7am–midnight) in the Al Saqr Business Tower, is a perennial favourite, while there is shisha at **Al Safadi** (www.alsafadi.ae; Sat–Wed 8am–1.30am, Thu–Fri until 2.30am) in Al Kawakeb Building A. Places on the opposite, western, side of the road include the chic **Japengo Café** (daily 7am–1am, Fri–Sat until 2 am) in the Oasis Tower. It offers an international menu with an Asian fusion twist.

View of Dubai Fountain from Burj Khalifa

The astonishing size of the Burj Khalifa and its distinctively tapering outline is hard to grasp close up – the whole thing is best appreciated from a distance, from where you can properly appreciate the tower's jaw-dropping size, and the degree to which it dwarfs the surrounding high-rises, many of which are considerable structures in their own right. The simple but elegant design (by Adrian Smith of the Chicago architectural firm Skidmore, Owings and Merrill) is based on an unusual Y-shaped ground plan, with the three projecting wings being gradually stepped back as the tower rises, so that the entire building becomes progressively narrower as it gains height.

The easiest way to visit the tower is to take the expensive trip up to the misleadingly named 'At the Top' observation deck (on floor 124, although there are actually 160 floors). Tours leave from the ticket counter in the lower-ground floor of the Dubai Mall. Tickets cost from 135Dhs (levels 124 and 125) if pre-booked online at www.burjkhalifa.ae or pre-purchased at the ticket counter. A premium experience also includes a visit to level 148 (Dhs 370–525). If you want to go up without a prior reservation, you'll have to fork out heftier sums than those above. In any case, you should book well in advance because there is usually a wait of at least a week to go up the tower.

AROUND DOWNTOWN DUBAI

Immediately below the Burj Khalifa lies the spectacular **Dubai Fountain ㉑**. Standing in the shadow of the world's tallest building, this is, appropriately enough, the world's largest fountain: 275m (900ft) long, illuminated with over 6,000 lights and with water-canons capable of shooting jets of water up to 150m (490ft) high. The fountain springs into action after dark, shooting choreographed jets of water into the air which 'dance' in time to a range of Arabic, Hindi and classical songs, while multicoloured lights play to-and-fro across the watery plumes. 'Performances' are staged every 30 minutes between 6pm and 11pm every day in the evening, and in the afternoon at 1pm and 1.30pm (Sat–Thu) and at 1.30pm and 2pm (Fri). Shows can be watched for free from anywhere around the lake.

Immediately beyond the fountain and lake lies yet another record-breaker, the gargantuan **Dubai Mall ㉒** (www.thedubai mall.com; retailers Sun–Wed 10am–11pm, Thu–Sat until midnight), covering a total area of 12 million sq ft (1 million sq metres), with over 1200 shops spread across four floors, making it easily the world's largest mall measured by total area (although other malls contain more retail space). Flagship outlets include branches of the famous Galleries Lafayette and Bloomingdale's department stores, a huge branch of the Japanese bookseller Kinokuniya and an offshoot of London's famous Hamley's toy store. There is also a vast selection of

The decorative interior of the Jumeirah Grand Mosque dome

upmarket designer stores, mainly concentrated along 'Fashion Avenue', complete with its own catwalk and Armani café, and a pretty Gold Souk with attractive Arabian design.

The mall is also home to the **Dubai Aquarium and Underwater Zoo** (www.thedubaiaquarium.com; Thu–Sat 10am–midnight, Sun–Wed until 11pm). The aquarium's most notable feature is the spectacular 'viewing panel', towering over the shops by the main entrance to the mall: a huge, floor-to-ceiling transparent acrylic panel filled with an extraordinary array of marine life, ranging from sand-tiger sharks and stingrays to colourful shoals of tiny tropical fish. All this can be seen for free from the mall; inside, the Underwater Zoo is more likely to appeal to children than adults, with displays themed after various different types of marine habitat and featuring an array of wildlife ranging from tiny cichlids and poison-dart frogs through to otters, penguins and seals.

Shops apart, the mall also boasts a host of other leisure attractions. Children will enjoy the state-of-the-art SEGA Republic theme park and KidZania, while there is also an Olympic-size ice rink.

Heading back to the lake at the back of the mall, a small footbridge leads across to the chintzy 'Old Town' development: a large swathe of low-rise, sand-coloured buildings with traditional

Moorish styling. On the far side of the footbridge lies the cute little **Souk al Bahar** ('Souk of the Sailor'; www.soukalbahar.ae; Sat–Thu 10am–10pm, Fri 2–10pm), a small, Arabian-themed mall specialising in traditional handicrafts and independent fashion. Restaurants line the waterfront terrace outside, offering peerless views of Burj Khalifa and Dubai Fountain after dark.

On the far side of the Souk al Bahar stands **The Palace** hotel, its sumptuous Moorish-style facade and richly decorated interior offering a surreal contrast to the futuristic needle of the Burj Khalifa rising directly behind.

If you fancy a respite from the high-rise architecture, the lush **Safa Park** (Thu–Sat 8am–11pm, Sun–Wed 8am–10pm; Tue women only) near Interchange No. 2 on the Arabian Gulf side of Sheikh Zayed Road, offers plenty of grass and fresh air and is a popular venue for walkers and joggers. Since 2016, the **Dubai Canal** going through the Safa Park has linked Dubai Creek with the Arabian Gulf. With its romantic footbridges and neighbouring cafés the development breathes new life into the area. Along the canal, a new business district – the **Business Bay** – is also being constructed. Although works have been largely stalled in recent years, the area is home to the world's second tallest hotel; the JW Marriott Marquis was completed in 2012.

In 2016, another landmark development was opened in Downtown Dubai – the **Dubai Opera House** (www.dubaiopera.com) designed by world-acclaimed architect Zaha Hadid, whose project – styled on traditional Arabian sailing vessels –rivals that of the famous Opera House in Sydney. The multi-use venue is a focal point for the Dubai new cultural centre, the Opera District, which is easily accessed from **Sheikh Mohammed bin Rashid Boulevard**, a vibrant street lined with numerous restaurants and cafés that encircles Burj Khalifa, the Dubai Fountain and the Dubai Mall.

JUMEIRAH

Running parallel to Sheikh Zayed Road, Dubai's beach-fringed coastline begins just west of the old city centre, running to the border at the port and free-trade zone at Jebel Ali, some 32km (20 miles) distant. The easternmost stretch of beach can be found in the upmarket but low-key suburb of **Jumeirah**. The closest coastal suburb to the old city centre, this sleepy area was where many expatriates settled in the 1960s, '70s and '80s, and the suburb remains popular with wealthy expat businessmen and their wives – caricatured in urban legend as 'Jumeirah Janes', who spend their days tanning by the pool of a private club and lunching with friends.

Jumeirah's main artery is **Jumeirha Road** (also known as 'Beach Road'), which runs dead straight down the coast for some 15km (9 miles) from Union House near Dubai Dry Docks to the Madinat Jumeirah resort. Lying between Jumeirah Road and Sheikh Zayed Road, roughly parallel to both, is Al Wasl Road. When traffic is heavy on Jumeirah Road, as it can be around Mercato Mall on Thursday evenings, Al Wasl Road provides an alternative route, and vice versa.

The major tourist sight in Jumeirah is **Jumeirah Mosque ㉓**, at the city end of Jumeirah Road. Built in the medieval Fatimid-style between 1975 and 1978, Jumeirah Mosque is the only one in the city that non-Muslims are permitted to enter: the Sheikh Mohammed Centre for Cultural Understanding (tel: 04 353 6666; www.cultures.ae) arranges tours four days a week, starting at 9am (Sat) or 10.30am (Sun, Tue–Thu). Tours begin with entertaining and informative talks by a local Emirati guide on traditional religious practices, after which the floor is thrown open to questions, offering visitors a chance to quiz the guide on any aspect of the local culture's way of life. There is no need to book, but you

View of Dubai Marina from the beach

should be at the mosque 15 minutes before the tour starts and buy your ticket outside.

Nearby **Union House**, a modest, round, glass-walled structure, is where the ruling sheikhs of six Emirates declared the UAE an independent federation on 2 December 1971 (the seventh emirate, Ras Al Khaimah joined in 1972). It is a short walk from Jumeirah Mosque towards Dubai Dry Docks – look for the giant flagpole with the UAE flag along Jumeirah Road. The area around Jumeirah Mosque, with its myriad cafés and small malls, is one of Dubai's nearest equivalents to an urban village. Across the road from Jumeirah Mosque, Palm Strip Mall has the original **Japengo Café** (offshoots of which can now be found across the Gulf), while just a short walk away on the mosque side of the road is the ever-popular **Lime Tree Café** (www.thelimetree cafe.com; daily 7.30am–6pm), another Dubai original, and the city's archetypal expat hangout.

Continuing west along Jumeirah Road, **Jumeirah Centre Mall** (www.jumeirahcentre.net) is home to the original Magrudy's book shop (https://magrudy.com), which now has branches in malls citywide, and the coffee shop **Gerard**, a Dubai institution that has survived the influx of American and European franchise cafés and is particularly popular with young Emiratis. The next mall along, **Jumeirah Plaza**, has a **Dôme** café that's popular with locals and

Jumeirah Beach Park

expats alike (www.dome uae.com). Across the road, the more modern **Village Mall** is the best in the area, with a small but rewarding clutch of shops including S*uce, one of the city's best places for independent designer labels (http://shopatsauce.com), and another of Dubai's popular **Shakespeare and Co.** cafés (www.shakespeare-and-co.com), with chintzy décor and outdoor seating in winter.

Close by, **Jumeirah Open Beach** (also known as 'Russian Beach') next to Dubai Marine Beach Resort and Spa and behind The Village Mall offers one of Dubai's biggest swathes of free sand. Bathers should beware, however: while the waters may look calm, Jumeirah has notoriously strong rip tides that can drag even experienced swimmers out to sea. While swimming trunks and bikinis are acceptable on the beach, bathers should cover up for visits to the cafés and malls on nearby Jumeirah Road.

Just over a kilometre further down the road is the decidedly old-style **Dubai Zoo** ㉔ (daily except Tue 10am–6pm, Nov–Feb until 5.30pm). Founded in 1967, the zoo is the oldest on the Arabian peninsula, and it is very much looking its age, with overcrowded pens housing a motley assortment of animals, almost all of which arrived at the zoo having been taken from smugglers apprehended by UAE customs officials. Amongst their number are giraffes, tigers, lions, chimps and brown bears, as well as local species, including Arabian wolves and oryx.

SOUTHERN JUMEIRAH

Further southwest along Jumeirah Road is the somewhat cheerier, Italian-inspired **Mercato Mall** ㉕ (http://mercato shoppingmall.com; most shops and restaurants: Sun–Wed 10am–10pm, Thu–Sat until midnight), whose faux Tuscan and Venetian architecture has made it a tourist attraction in its own right. Inside, the large central atrium, with its glass roof, old clock, coffee shop and escalators, resembles a 19th-century railway station.

A couple of kilometres further down the road, the recently refurbished **Jumeirah Beach Park** ㉖ (daily 7.30am–10pm, Thu–Fri until 11pm) is by far the nicest public beach in the city. Entrance costs Dhs15, giving you access to a fine stretch of white sand (manned by lifeguards) backed by attractive gardens plus assorted cafés, kids' play areas and barbecue stands.

A short inland hop from Jumeirah Beach Park, a residential neighbourhood between Jumeirah Road and Al Wasl Road is the unlikely location of one of the Arabian Gulf's most significant archaeological sites: the **Jumeirah Archaeological Site** (Sun–Thu 9am–2pm), where the ruins of a port town dating back more than 1,000 years have been uncovered by archaeologists since 1969. The original settlement, strategically positioned on the ancient trade route between Mesopotamia and Oman, dates back to the pre-Islamic Sassanid era, which ended in the 7th century AD. The site was built upon and expanded by the Abbasids in the first two or three centuries of the Islamic era and is today one of the largest and most important early Islamic sites in the Gulf. Excavated ruins include the foundations of several houses, includ-ing the Sassanid-era governor's palace, market buildings, a large caravanserai in which travellers would meet and do business, and a small mosque, although unfortunately they are all extremely fragmentary, and unlikely to mean much unless you are a trained archaeologist.

Jumeirah's other sight of historic interest is the more recent **Majlis Ghorfat Umm al Sheif** ㉗ (Sun–Thu 7.30am–2.30pm), Sheikh Rashid's modest two-storey summer resort made of coral stone and gypsum. Built in 1955, when this part of the coast was far removed from the city on the creek, the *majlis* was used by Sheikh Rashid, father of the current ruler, as a meeting house before becoming a police station for a time in the 1960s. A small museum now, the grounds have an example of the traditional *falaj* system of irrigation and a *barasti* (palm frond) structure with a working wind-tower. It is located on Street 17, off Jumeirah Road – look for the brown heritage-site signs between Jumeirah Beach Park and Burj Al Arab.

Just 4 kilometres (2.5 miles) off the coast from the adjacent Jumeirah Beach Park, the **World Islands**, 300 artificial islands in the shape of a world map, have been in development since 2003. When completed, the islands will serve as residential sites, resorts, shopping and entertainment venues. A man-made archipelago in the shape of the solar system was also planned for the future, to be located next to the World Islands. Due to the economic slowdown, however, there is no completion date planned for the Universe.

Continuing south down Sheikh Zayed Road, it is a further 10km (6 miles) to the landmark **Mall of the Emirates** ㉘ (www.mallof theemirates.com; retailers: daily 10am–10pm, Thu–Fri until midnight, restaurants: Sun–Wed 10am–11pm, Thu–Sat until midnight). Formerly the largest in the city, until being eclipsed by the Dubai Mall, the Mall of the Emirates is still one of the best places to shop in the city – and is less exhaustingly huge than the Dubai

Mall. Mall of the Emirates has almost 500 shops, covering pretty much every retail option.

Shopping aside, the Mall of the Emirates is best known as the home of **Ski Dubai** (Sun–Wed 10am–11pm, Thu 10am–midnight, Fri 9am–midnight, Sat 9am–11pm), the first indoor ski resort in the Middle East, complete with regular falls of artificial snow. This is the world's largest indoor snow park, with an alpine ski slope offering five runs of varying levels of difficulty – a truly surreal experience in the middle of the desert, and a great place to cool off when the mercury is touching 48°C (118°F) outside.

A short drive east of the Mall of the Emirates, on the desert side of the highway near Interchange No. 4, the functional **Gold and Diamond Park** lacks the atmosphere of the city's traditional souks but offers some of the cheapest gold and precious stones in the city – diamonds are a particularly good buy (www.goldand diamondpark.com; Sat–Thu 10am–10pm, Fri 4–10pm).

UMM SUQEIM

The Majlis Ghorfat Umm Al Sheef marks the southern limits of Jumeirah proper, after which you enter the adjacent suburb of **Umm Suqeim** (although the entire area is usually referred to as Jumeirah). Here you'll find three of Dubai's most famous modern

Madinat Jumeirah resort: 21st-century luxury in traditional style

landmarks: the wave-shaped Jumeirah Beach Hotel, the spectac-ular Madinat Jumeirah complex and the iconic Burj Al Arab hotel.

BURJ AL ARAB AND AROUND

Without a doubt, the jewel of the Dubai coast is the **Burj Al Arab** hotel ❷❾ (literally 'Tower of the Arabs'), the city's best-known landmark, which since its opening in December 1999 has gained an iconic status similar to that of the Big Ben or the Eiffel Tower, especially in the Middle East. The 321-m- (1,053-ft-) high structure, shaped like a sail to complement the 'wave' design of the nearby Jumeirah Beach Hotel, dominates the surrounding residential neighbourhood and can be seen from virtually any point on the Dubai coast. A seven-star hotel, built on its own man-made island and comprising 202 two-storey suites, each with its own butler, Burj Al Arab restricts access to hotel guests or those who have booked a table at one of its restaurants. These include the fabulous Al Muntaha (literally 'The Highest'), 200m (656ft) above the Arabian Gulf, with breathtaking views of the coast.

Best viewed from the public beach to the north or from various vantage points around the Madinat Jumeirah complex, the most distinctive feature of 'the Burj' is the double-skinned, Teflon-coated, woven glass-fibre screen facade, which is white by day and illuminated by coloured lights at night. The space-age helicopter pad jutting out from the top floor like a mini *Starship Enterprise* was famously used as a practice driving range by Tiger Woods and as a tennis court by Roger Federer and Andre Agassi.

Below the towering Burj Al Arab, next to the Jumeirah Beach Hotel, is **Wild Wadi Water Park** (daily Sept–Oct, Mar–May 10am–7pm, Nov–Feb 10am–6pm, Jun–Aug 10am–8pm), which has 30

⊙ BRAND NEW OLD

The Madinat Jumeirah resort on the Jumeirah coast is a reimagining of what Dubai could have looked like in previous centuries if builders of those times had access to modern construction materials and techniques, not to mention larger budgets. It mixes the wind-tower houses of the Al Fahidi Historical Neighbourhood with the modest former palace in Shindagha and the souks of old Dubai, and stretches them upwards and outwards.

Designer Thanu Boonyawatana likened his approach to that of a movie special-effects wizard who, with the aid of computer-generated imagery, is able to recreate ancient Greece or Rome for cinema audiences: 'We thought, "What if in ancient UAE or ancient Oman they had the money we have now and the technology we have now? What would they have built?" We built what they might have built with the resources available to us.'

Hookahs at the Souk Madinat Jumeirah

rides and attractions, including the Jumeirah Sceirah, the tallest free-fall slide outside North America, and the Wipeout Flow Rider surf pool, where budding surfers can ride a continuously breaking 3-m- (10-ft-) high wave. For an alternative and completely free way of getting wet, head to **Umm Suqeim Public Beach**, on the city side of the Burj Al Arab hotel. The view of the Burj Al Arab from this stretch of beach is stunning, particularly at sunset.

A stone's throw south along the coast, the splendid **Madinat Jumeirah** ㉚ (literally 'Jumeirah City') resort takes its inspiration from the wind-tower houses of Al Fahidi Historical Neighbourhood, but modern construction techniques allow for taller, more impressive structures, making the resort a fabulous reinterpretation of traditional Arabian architecture. A definite 'must see' for any visitor, Madinat Jumeirah has two luxury hotels – Mina A'Salam (literally 'Port of Peace') and Al Qasr ('The Palace'), both of which have jaw-droppingly beautiful interior décor and a number of licensed restaurants and bars in idyllic sea-view settings that are open to non-guests (see page 135). The resort also provides accommodation at the luxurious Malakiya Villas and Dar Al Masyaf two-storey houses. A network of canals, serviced by *abra* water taxis, links the hotels and wind-tower summer houses with the souk and various waterfront restaurants.

Madinat Jumeirah is also home to the delightful covered market, **Souk Madinat Jumeirah** (daily 10am–11pm), which despite its relatively recent construction manages to convey an authentic atmosphere. As well as various antiques shops, clothing boutiques and handicraft stalls, the souk has a number of bars, licensed restaurants and cafés that spread onto picturesque terraces.

THE PALM JUMEIRAH AND DUBAI MARINA

South of Madinat Jumeirah in the suburb of Al Sufouh, a multi-lane highway branches off the coastal highway to head out to sea and the remarkable **Palm Jumeirah**. Visible from space, the Palm Jumeirah is one of three ambitious palm-tree shaped land-reclamation projects off the Dubai coast.

As its name implies, the island is designed in the form of a palm tree, with the main road running down the central 'trunk', a series of sixteen 'fronds' spreading out to either side, covered in luxury villas, and an outer breakwater lined with upmarket hotels. Unfortunately, you can only really appreciate the unique layout of the island from the air; from the ground, the whole thing looks like suburban clutter, while the architecture along the main trunk road is decidedly humdrum, at least until you approach the far end of the island, and the grandiose Atlantis resort hoves into view ahead.

ATLANTIS

At the far end of the Palm, the vast **Atlantis resort** ❸❶ rears into view above the seafront (www.atlantisthepalm.com). The resort is an almost identikit copy of its sister establishment, the Atlantis Paradise Island resort in the Bahamas, with the addition of the few discrete Islamic touches, and looks like some enormous Disney palace. Inside, the hotel is as unabashedly over-the-top as one would expect. Entering the main foyer, you are confronted by Dale Chihuly's extraordinary sculptural installation in the lobby – a towering glass sculpture looking like a huge waterfall of deep-frozen noodles. Corridors stretch away in either direction, lined with fat gold columns and vast chandeliers, while a floor-to-ceiling viewing panel offers spectacular glimpses into the vast aquarium of the hotel's Lost Chambers.

Atlantis boasts a host of (expensive) in-house attractions. Inside the hotel itself, the kooky **Lost Chambers** (daily 10am–10pm) purports to consist of the remains of the legendary city of Atlantis itself, featuring a sequence of underwater halls and tunnels, dotted with specially constructed 'ruins'. This is Dubai at its most shamelessly kitsch, although you may enjoy the sheer absurdity of the idea, while the 65,000-odd resident fish, both large and small, swimming around the submerged faux-classical remains, are impressive.

In the grounds outside you'll find the resort's spectacular **Aquaventure Waterpark** (daily 10am–5.30pm), home to a pulse-quickening selection of water-coasters, speedslides and power-jets, plus the dramatic 'Ziggurat'

Coastal growth

Dubai's natural coastline is 72km (45 miles) long, but land reclamation projects are extending it by an incredible 1,500km (932 miles), which is longer than the natural coastline of the entire UAE.

Atlantis resort

and 'Leap of Faith' waterslide, which drops those brave enough to tackle it, at stomach-churning speeds, down into a plastic tunnel in the middle of a lagoon full of sharks. There are also various gentler activities for kids (including a children's play area), while visitors can also use the fine stretch of private beach next door. The adjacent **Dolphin Bay** offers the chance to swim with the hotel's troupe of resident bottlenose dolphins.

DUBAI MARINA

Past the turn-off to the Palm rise the massed buildings of the vast new Dubai Marina development (or 'New Dubai', as it is sometimes called). This entire district is effectively a brand new city-within-the-city: a swathe of densely packed skyscrapers, which mushroomed out of the desert with magical rapidity within a five year period. Even by Dubai standards, the speed and scale of the development here takes the breath away,

The gleaming white towers of Dubai Marina

especially for those who remember this part of Dubai in its pre-2005 days, when the entire area was little more than untouched desert, bar a modest line of hotels fringing the coast.

These upmarket beachside hotels remain the Marina's principal tourist draw, lining the long expanse of fine white-sand beach on the western side of the area. The hotel strip begins at its eastern end with the Arabian-themed **One&Only Royal Mirage** ㉜, one of the city's loveliest hotels, followed in rapid succession by the Meridien Mina Seyahi and Westin hotels.

Past here the main road drops over the sea inlet leading into Dubai Marina itself to reach **The Walk** ㉝, an attractive pedestrianized promenade running along the back of the beach, dotted with dozens of cafés and restaurants. The Marina itself is a man-made sea inlet, around 1.5km (1 mile) long, with many luxury yachts and expensive speedboats, all hemmed in by a forest of skyscrapers. It is an impressive sight, although the haphazard layout of the entire area, with random high-rises crammed pell-mell into every available space, serves as a chastening memorial to the super-fuelled property boom of the mid-noughties, from which the city is still recovering.

IBN BATTUTA MALL

Some 4km (2.5 miles) south of the Marina lies the quirky **Ibn Battuta Mall** ❸ (www.ibnbattutamall.com; daily 10am–10pm, Thu–Sat until midnight), situated in something of a no-man's land at the far southern end of the city, close to the sprawling industrial works and container docks of the Jebel Ali Free Trade Zone. The mall is one of the city's most outlandish but engaging attractions, inspired by the travels of the famous Moroccan wanderer Ibn Battuta, with different sections themed after six of the many countries and regions he visited – Morocco, Andalusia, Tunisia, Persia, India and China – all designed with Dubai's characteristic mix of whimsy extravagance and high kitsch.

AWAY FROM THE COAST

RAS AL KHOR WILDLIFE SANCTUARY

Close to Nad Al Sheba, the tidal lagoon at the top of Dubai Creek is home to the UAE's largest bird sanctuary, **Ras al Khor Wildlife Sanctuary** ❸ (hides accessible Sat–Thu 7.30am–5.30pm), which can host up to 15,000 birds on a single winter's day, including between 1,000 and 1,500 migrant greater flamingos, which have been a protected species here since 1985. Other species that can be seen from the purpose-built viewing hides on Route 66 and Ras al Khor Road (Route 44) include Socotra cormorants, cream-coloured coursers and crab plovers.

Racing camels exercise year-round at Nad al Sheba

MEYDAN

Evidence of the seriousness with which Dubai takes its racing can be seen in the spectacular **Meydan Racecourse** ㊱ (www.meydan.ae) just south of Ras al Khor (see page 88). The racing season is held during the cooler winter months from November to March, culminating in the prestigious Dubai World Cup, the world's richest horse race, with prize money of $10 million. Race-meets are also a major feature on the city's social calendar, attracting a lively crowd of Emiratis and expats, although no betting is allowed.

DUBAILAND

The vast **Dubailand** development has become the major symbol of Dubai's over-reaching ambition. Occupying a huge swathe of land on the southern side of the city, Dubailand was slated (according to plans announced at its launch in 2003) to become the planet's largest and most spectacular tourist development, with an extraordinary mix of theme parks and sporting and leisure facilities, covering a staggering 280 sq km (108 sq miles) – twice the size of the Walt Disney World Resort in Florida. Due to the financial crisis, work on the many parts of the development was stalled, but resumed in mid-2013, and it is now scheduled for completion by 2020.

Parts of the development, however, have been up and running in the meantime, including the **Dubai Autodrome** (www.dubaiautodrome.com), a 5.39-km (3.3-mile) Formula One-standard motor-racing circuit which hosts rounds of the FIA GT Championship and **Dubai Sports City** ❸❼ (www.dsc.ae), complete with international cricket stadium and Els golf course. It is also home to Butch Harmon School of Golf, ICC Global Cricket Academy and

⊘ RELIGIOUS TOLERANCE

According to the Sheikh Mohammed Centre for Cultural Understanding (see page 37), 'Cultural and religious diversity has made the Emirates probably the most open and tolerant country within the region. Dubai and the UAE in general are liberal in allowing foreigners to maintain their own religious practices and lifestyles.'

Although Emiratis are Muslims and the legal system that applies to locals and foreigners alike is based on Islamic Sharia Law, the Dubai government allows people of other faiths to gather for worship, as long as they don't proselytise Muslims. A number of Christian churches have been established on land provided by the rulers on the Bur Dubai side of the Creek. As Friday is the local weekend, most churches have main services then – Sunday is a normal working day.

rugby and football fields. The most recent addition is the **Miracle Garden** (www.dubaimiraclegarden.com; Sun–Thu 9am–9pm, Fri–Sat 9am–11pm). Opened in 2013, it is full of blooming flowers meticulously arranged in myriad designs that change each season, and as many Dubai projects are world-unique, this is perhaps the gaudiest example of garden kitsch on earth. Close by on Emirates Road is **Global Village** ❸❽ (http://globalvillage.ae; mid-Nov–mid-April Sat–Wed 4pm–midnight, Thu–Fri and holidays 4pm–1am), a combination of funfair and international retail park, with numerous European, African and Asian nations represented by elaborate pavilions. Horse riding is possible at the Al Sahra Equestrian Centre, situated within the whole complex.

DAY TRIPS

THE DESERT

A trip into the **desert** is highly recommended for all visitors to Dubai. The dunes that begin on the outskirts of the city continue into Abu Dhabi Emirate and eventually merge with the fabled Rub Al Khali, or Empty Quarter, the largest sand desert in the world. But visitors needn't travel far from Dubai to experience towering dunes, and pretty much every tour agent in the city offers popular (if touristy) half-day 'desert safaris', featuring some dune-bashing (driving at speed over the sands) followed by a visit to a desert camp for various entertainments including belly-dancing, henna-painting, camel-riding and so on. Most companies head out to the dunes around 'Big Red', a mammoth mountain of sand along the road to Hatta.

Several companies also offer longer and more rewarding desert excursions. Popular destinations include the Dubai Desert Conservation Reserve, in which herds of rare Arabian oryx roam

free; Fossil Rock, where the fossils of marine creatures can be found on a rocky outcrop, confirming that this area was once the ocean floor; and Hatta Pools, cool mountain springs in the foot-hills of the Hajar range near the UAE border with Oman.

HATTA

The Dubai enclave of **Hatta** ㊴, on the highway 115km (71 miles) from the city, can be reached by car in around an hour. Hatta's appeal lies in the contrast of its oasis greenery and rugged mountain backdrop, but its main visitor attraction is undoubtedly **Hatta Heritage Village** (Sat–Thu 7.30am–8.30pm, Fri 2.30–8.30pm), which traces the history of the settlement from its formation some 3,000 years ago to the 19th century and has examples of 30 traditional structures, from a fortress built by Sheikh Maktoum Bin Hasher Al Maktoum in 1896 to small mountain dwellings that wouldn't look out of place on the islands off the Scottish coast. The defensive watchtowers on either side of the heritage village offer superb views of the museum and the modern town. No day trip to Hatta would be complete without a refreshing drink, or perhaps a meal, beside the pool at the **Hatta Fort Hotel**, a popular weekend destination among Dubai's expatriate community.

SHARJAH

On the coast north of Dubai lies **Sharjah** ⑩, once the most important town on the Trucial Coast, but now overshadowed by its more glamorous neighbour. Nevertheless, Sharjah has a number of attractions to justify the trip out from Dubai. In the centre of town, the Creekside **heritage area** is home to several small museums and the pretty little Al Arsa Souk, while just down the road lie the old city **fort**, the **Sharjah Art Gallery** and the outstanding new **Sharjah Museum of Islamic Civilization** (www.sharjahmuseums.ae; Sat–Thu 8am–8pm, Fri 4–8pm). Slightly out from the centre, the landmark **Blue Souk** is home to a good selection of carpet and handicrafts shops, while the nearby aviation-themed **Al Mahatta Museum** (www.sharjah museums.ae; Sat–Thu 8am–8pm, Fri 4–8pm) occupies the site of the former airport, established in 1932 to serve the pioneering Imperial Airways route between Croydon, England and Australia.

AL AIN

The attractive city of Al Ain – the UAE's largest inland settlement – offers a rewarding day trip from Dubai, an easy 90-minute journey by car or bus along the swift E66 highway. The greenest city in the UAE, Al Ain grew up around the string of seven oases that survive to this day; the largest, right in the heart of the city, makes for a beautifully peaceful and shaded walk along narrow lanes threading their way between endless

Beach resort in Fujairah

lines of date palms. The city is also famous for its fine collection of traditional mudbrick forts, including the striking Al Jahili Fort and the rustic little Sultan Zayed Fort, which stands next to the Al Ain National Museum (Tue–Sun 8.30am–7.30pm, Fri from 3pm). Nearby, the lively Camel Souk (daily 6am–7pm) is also worth a visit, as is the breezy summit of the craggy Jebel Hafeet mountain, rising to the south of the city.

THE EAST COAST

On the east coast of the UAE, between one and two hours' drive from Dubai, the highway from Masafi to Fujairah passes **Bithnah Fort**, which in its mountain oasis setting is reminiscent of the great forts of northern Oman. **Fujairah** also has an imposing fortress with a mountain backdrop. The fort, attacked by British forces in colonial times, is believed to be the oldest in the UAE, the main part dating back 500 years.

Sheikh Zayed Grand Mosque in Abu Dhabi

The UAE's oldest mosque, built around 1446, is on the coast 38km (24 miles) north of Fujairah at **Badiyah** (non-Muslims usually allowed in outside prayer times). A short drive further north is the gorgeous **Al Aqah Beach ㊶**, a popular weekend retreat for Dubai residents, with a trio of upmarket hotels, including the landmark **Le Meridien al Aqah Beach Resort**. The clear, warm waters around nearby **Snoopy Island** are particularly popular with scuba divers.

ABU DHABI

A quick two-hour drive down the coast, the wealthy capital of the UAE, **Abu Dhabi ㊷** is trying to keep pace with its upstart neighbour Dubai. It offers a good selection of attractive beaches, swanky hotels and a growing number of the country's landmark attractions. The major sight here is the vast **Sheikh Zayed Mosque** (www.szgmc.gov.ae; Sat–Thu 9am–10pm, Fri

4.30–10pm; free admission and free guided tours in English), completed in 2007 and one of the largest and most lavishly decorated places of worship anywhere in the world.

The city's landmark development project of recent years has been the **Saadiyat Island Cultural District** (www.saadiyat. ae), a planned home to five major museums all designed by world-renowned architects. Jean Nouvel's **Louvre Abu Dhabi** (http://louvreabudhabi.ae), showcasing a fine collection of both Eastern and Western art, opened in 2017. The construction of Norman Foster's **Zayed National Museum** and Frank Ghery's **Guggenheim Abu Dhabi** (www.guggenheim.org/abu-dhabi) have not yet begun. There are works underway for the **Performing Arts Centre** by Zaha Hadid Architects and the **Maritime Museum** by Tadao Ando. All projects feature absolutely stunning architecture.

In the centre of town, the sprawling old **Qasr al Hosn** fort presents the history of the UAE (www.qasralhosn.ae, several exhibitions are closed for renovation), and each February live performances are held during the annual Qasr al Hosn Festival (www.qasralhosn.ae). There is also a very good state-of-the-art exhibition on Abu Dhabi's heritage mounted in the adjacent **Cultural Foundation** building (Sat–Thu 8am–10pm). The nearby **World Trade Centre** – a stunning, post-modern souk designed by Norman Foster – opened in 2014 (www.wtcad.ae; daily 10am–10pm, Sat–Sun until 11pm). Other interesting attractions include the well-presented **Heritage Village** (Sat–Thu 9am–4pm, Fri 3.30–9pm) and the old-fashioned **Al Bateen Dhow Yard**. On the outskirts of town, **Yas Island** (www.yasisland.ae) is the venue of the Abu Dhabi F1 Grand Prix and home to the thrills and spills of the **Ferrari World Theme Park** (www.ferrariworldabudhabi.com; daily 11am–8pm).

On a desert safari

WHAT TO DO

Dubai boasts attractions for all tastes. You can watch international entertainers and sporting champions perform, shop till you drop in the souks or air-conditioned malls, play on championship golf courses, or even ski on indoor slopes.

ORGANISED TOURS

Desert safari. Most 4x4 tours depart in the morning or late afternoon. Later tours are usually combined with a dune dinner and entertainment (belly dancing and henna body painting) after sunset at the tour company's torch-lit *bedu*-style desert camp.

Dhow cruise. A traditional way of experiencing Dubai Creek is by dhow, usually during an evening dinner cruise (see page 105)– tours are easily arranged through your hotel or any local tour operator. A more cost-effective and flexible option is to negotiate with an *abra* (water taxi) operator for your own tour of the Creek, which costs Dhs120 per hour per boat (irrespective of the number of people on it).

Air tours. A number of tour operators offer helicopter tours – Aerogulf (based at the international airport;

Ramadan

Remember that during the holy month of Ramadan, eating and drinking in public (which includes smoking and chewing gum) are forbidden during daylight hours, and although hotels serve guests food and drink in curtained-off areas, no alcohol is served anywhere until after dark. The city's nightlife also grinds to a halt: live music is banned and clubs close for the duration.

tel: 04 877 6120; www.aerogulfservices.com) are one of the best established. Prices are around $200 for a 15-minute flight. For hot-air ballooning over the desert contact Balloon Adventures Emirates (tel: 04 440 9827; www.ballooning.ae).

SPORT

PARTICIPANT SPORTS

Desert sports. Novel sports include sand-skiing and sand-boarding, which visitors can try on organised tours.

Golf. Dubai's most famous 18-hole courses are at the Emirates and Dubai Creek (both tel: 04 380 1234; www.dubaigolf.com) clubs. The Emirates' 7,211-yard Majlis is the venue for the Dubai Desert Classic, but newer courses such as the Montgomerie at Emirates Hills (tel: 04 390 5600; www.themontgomerie.com), designed by Colin Montgomerie, and the Arabian Ranches Golf Course (tel: 04 366 4700; www.arabianranchesgolfdubai.com), designed by Ian Baker-Finch with Nicklaus Design, are fast gaining international

---

⊘ SPA DAYS

Spa treatments are big business in Dubai. Most of the bigger hotels have spas – many of them offering lavish treatments in idyllic surroundings – Talise spas at the Burj Al Arab and Madinat Jumeirah, Amara spa at the Park Hyatt Hotel, Spa and Oriental Hammam at the One&Only Royal Mirage are four of the most memorable. There are also some independent, and more affordable places – Cleopatra's Spa in Wafi is one of the best, while some of the city's numerous nail bars (N Bar is the main chain) also offer assorted massages.

reputations. More recent additions include the 'desert links' style course at the Els Club at Dubai Sports City in Dubailand (tel: 04 425 1000; www.elsclubdubai.com), and the Jumeirah Golf Estates in Dubai Marina (tel: 04 818 2000; www.jumeirahgolfestates.com).

Dubai is home to the first indoor ski slope in the Middle East

Skiing. The Middle East's first indoor ski resort, Ski Dubai at Mall of the Emirates (www.mallofthe emirates.com, www.the playmania.com; Sun–Wed 10am–11pm, Thu 10am–midnight, Fri 9am–midnight, Sat 9am–11pm), has five ski runs of up to 400 metres on artificially produced snow, including the world's first indoor black run, and a Snow Park with a snowball-throwing gallery. The entry pass includes warm clothing, but not hats or gloves. Absolute beginners are not allowed on the slopes without first taking lessons at the Snow School.

Tennis. Most of Dubai's resort hotels have good-quality hard courts as part of their fitness-centre offerings. Dubai's premier tennis venue is the Dubai Tennis Stadium in Garhoud (tel: 04 282 4122). Courts are available to non-members on an hourly basis for a charge that includes use of the club's other facilities. There are public tennis courts in Safa Park (tel: 04 349 2111).

Watersports. The beachfront resort hotels are the easiest places to arrange watersports. All the marina beach hotels (apart from the Ritz-Carlton) have their own watersports

The Dubai World Cup is horse racing's richest prize

centres, with activities including windsurfing, sailing, kayaking, water-skiing, wakeboarding and parasailing. Local operators include Sky & Sea Adventure (tel: 04 399 9005; www.watersports dubai.com), who can be found at the Sheraton Jumeirah Beach and Hilton Jumeirah Resort. For offshore sailing try the Dubai Offshore Sailing Club (tel: 04 394 1669; www.dosc.ae). The centre for sailing on the coast is Dubai International Marine Club (DIMC) in Mina Seyahi (tel: 04 399 5777; http://dimc.ae).

SPECTATOR SPORTS

Golf. The Omega Dubai Desert Classic (www.omegadubaidesert classic.com) is a major tournament on the PGA European Tour, held annually in Jan/Feb at the Emirates Golf Club. The four-day tournament attracts the biggest names in the sport – former winners include Ernie Els, Tiger Woods and Stephen Gallacher.

Horse racing. The racing season at Meydan Racecourse (www.meydan.ae) runs between November and March, with afternoon and evening races (mainly on Thursdays, Friday and sometimes Saturdays) culminating in the richest race day in the world, the US$10 million Dubai World Cup (www.dubai worldcup.com). See http://emiratesracing.com for details of forthcoming events.

Rugby. The Dubai Rugby Sevens (www.dubairugby7s.com), part of the IRB Sevens World Series, has grown to rival the Hong Kong Sevens in terms of the atmosphere around its 22,000-seat main pitch. The three-day event is held in late November/early December at the purpose-built The Sevens stadium on Al Ain Road, past Dubailand.

Tennis. The two-week Dubai Duty Free Tennis Championships (www.dubaidutyfreetennischampionships.com), at the Dubai Tennis Stadium in late February/early March, consists of separate,

⊘ THE RACING MAKTOUMS

Dubai's ruling family has become synonymous with international horse racing, thanks mostly to the success of the Godolphin stable (www.godolphin.com), established by Sheikh Mohammed and his brother Sheikh Hamdan in 1994 and named after Godolphin Arabian, a horse that was taken from the Yemeni desert to Europe in the early 18th century to become one of the three founding stallions of the modern thoroughbred.

The stable has trained such greats as Lammtarra, Swain, Daylami and Dubai Millennium. Typically, after a winter in Dubai, the Godolphin team heads to Europe, where its horses are stabled for the summer in Newmarket, the English town where Sheikh Mohammed is said to have acquired his love for horse racing in the 1960s while studying in nearby Cambridge. From Newmarket, the horses travel the world, to be ridden by the world's top jockeys, competing in the stable's distinctive blue silks.

On top of their Godolphin interests, the Maktoums also have private studs. In 1997, the late Sheikh Maktoum was the most successful owner in Europe, with group wins in five countries.

back-to-back women's WTA and men's ATP tournaments and attracts the world's top players. The annual ITF Al Habtoor Tennis Challenge, held at the Habtoor Grand Resort and Spa in Mina Seyahi, attracts the rising stars of the women's game.

Camel racing. The city's old camel racetrack at Nad al Sheba has now closed; the nearest camel-racing track is the Al Marmoum Camel RaceTrack, some 40km (25 miles) from Dubai, off exit 37 of the Al Ain road. Races are held from September to April, usually early in the morning around 6.30am.

Motorsport. Dubai Autodrome hosts the annual Dubai 24 Hour (a kind of local Le Mans; www.24hseries.com), but most of the action is in neighbouring Abu Dhabi, which hosts the annual Abu Dhabi F1 Grand Prix (www.formula1.com) as well as the Abu Dhabi Desert Challenge (www.abudhabidesertchallenge.com), an FIA-sanctioned off-road motor rally that covers some 2,000km (1,200 miles) of the desert interior in late March/early April.

Water sports. Sailing and rowing races for traditional boats are held off Mina Seyahi and on Dubai Creek several times a year. The Mina Seyahi coast also hosts two rounds of the UIM Class I World Powerboat Championship in November/December.

OUTDOOR PURSUITS

Desert safaris. See page 125.

Horse riding. Dubai Polo and Equestrian Club (tel: 04 361 8111; www.poloclubdubai.com) at Arabian Ranches offers desert rides and lessons. Other venues include Emirates Equestrian Centre (tel: 04 558 7656; www.emiratesequestriancentre.com), out in the desert not far from the Bab al Shams hotel.

Quad biking. For quad biking in the desert dunes, head for the cluster of small activity centres some 50km (31 miles) from the city, on Route 44 to Hatta.

Scuba diving. The Pavilion Dive Centre (tel: 04 406 8828) at the Jumeirah Beach Hotel offers a range of on-site PADI courses and introductory dives, plus dives to nearby wrecks and one- to three-day excursions to Musandam. Al Boom Diving (tel: 04 342 2993; www.alboomdiving.com) operates five dive centres in Dubai, and one at the Al Aqah Méridien hotel in Fujairah, offering a range of PADI courses and dives, plus Musandam excursions.

SHOPPING

With thriving souks, modern malls and the annual Dubai Shopping Festival (DSF; www.visitdubaishoppingfestival.com), which starts in January, Dubai is the proverbial shopper's paradise.

WHERE TO BUY

Souks. Dubai's most famous souk is the Gold Souk in Deira. Nearby is the Spice Souk, where frankincense and saffron can be purchased. Across the Creek, Bur Dubai Souk is the place for textiles. Generally, most shops open Sat–Thu 10am–1pm and 4–10pm, Fri 4–10pm. Bargaining is expected and shoppers should always ask for the 'best price'. The down-at-heel Karama Souk remains popular, thanks to its vast quantities

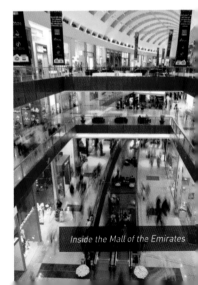
Inside the Mall of the Emirates

of designer fakes, cheap clothes and souvenirs. For a modern remake of the traditional Arabian souk, head either to the lovely Souk Madinat Jumeirah or the opulent new Khan Murjan Souk, both of which boast lavish décor and an Arabian Nights atmosphere – although prices are high.

Malls. Dubai's ultra-modern malls offer comfortable air-conditioned shopping, often amidst spectacular surroundings. Opening hours are generally daily 10am–10pm, and until midnight on Thursday, Friday and Saturday, though some are closed on Friday mornings. Prices are fixed.

For pure retail excess, the supersized Dubai Mall (www.thedubaimall.com) has by far the biggest selection of shops, while there are also shops galore at other major malls such as the Mall of the Emirates on Sheikh Zayed Road in Al Barsha (www.malloftheemirates.com). There are plenty of smaller malls too, including the exclusive Emirates Towers Boulevard and the chain of malls lining the northern end of Jumeirah Road.

Dubai's malls get particularly busy during the annual Dubai Shopping Festival in January, when shops across the city offer discounts and promotions, backed up by a lively programme of mall-based prize draws and entertainments. Dubai Summer Surprises (June–July) is another shopping-centred festival, with a similar range of discounts and in-mall entertainment designed to lure in punters during the hot summer months.

Dubai Shopping Festival

The month-long Dubai Shopping Festival (DSF; www.visitdubaishoppingfestival.com) was established in 1996. As many as over four million visitors attend this retail extravaganza, which usually starts in January.

WHAT TO BUY

Gold. Deira's famous Gold Souk is the focus of Dubai's

roaring gold trade, although there are plenty of dedicated gold shops nearby, opposite the Gold Souk bus station and in the southern city near Mall of the Emirates at the Gold and Diamond Park. Items are priced by weight according to the daily gold price, although bargaining is essential.

Be prepared to bargain at the Gold Souk

Carpets. The greatest concentration of carpet shops is in Deira Tower on Baniyas Square in Deira, while there are also carpet shops in most of the main malls (Emad Carpets and the Persian Carpet House are the main chains; www.pch. ae), although prices are significantly higher. The best buys are to be had at 'Carpet Oasis' during the annual shopping festival in January (check the local press or online for venue details). The Blue Souk in Sharjah also has some excellent carpet shops.

Fabrics. Thanks to its long-established links with India, Dubai is a great place for high-quality, low-cost fabrics. Bur Dubai Souk has a concentration of textile traders, while nearby Al Fahidi Street also has some very good shops. Pashminas are widely available.

Perfume. Distinctive Arabian scents are available from Ajmal Perfumes (www.ajmalperfume.com) and Arabian Oud (www.arabianoud.com), which have branches in many of the city's major malls. Alternatively, head for the Perfume Souk

The Skyview bar at the top of the Burj Al Arab

in Deira. Many places (including Ajmal) offer the chance to mix your own bespoke scents.

Souvenirs. There are souvenir shops in pretty much all the main malls in Dubai. For traditional Arabian artefacts (coffeepots, *shisha* pipes, framed *khanjar* daggers and so on) look out for branches of Al Jaber Gallery (www.aljabergallery.ae) and Pride of Kashmir (http://prideofkashmir.com). The best selection of souvenir shops can be found in Souk Madinat Jumeirah and Khan Murjan Souk – items for sale here are generally of a higher quality, albeit at above-average prices. The Camel Company (branches in malls citywide) does an entertaining line in cute toy camels and related merchandise (www.camelcompany.ae). Gallery One (also with outlets in malls across the city) does a superb range of limited-edition framed art photographs of the region, plus superior postcards (www.g-1.com).

For items crafted by Dubai-based artisans, browse among the stalls at Marina Market, held at Dubai Marina Mall Promenade (www.dubaimarinamall.com; Sat–Wed 10am–10pm, Thu–Fri 10am–noon).

Original artworks by local artists can be purchased at galleries across the city such as the Majlis (www.themajlisgallery.com) and XVA in the Al Fahidi Historical Neighbourhood (www.xvagallery.com) – expect to spend some serious cash.

ENTERTAINMENT

NIGHTLIFE

Dubai has a vibrant bar and nightclub scene. The busiest evenings tend to be on or around the local weekend (Wednesday, Thursday, Friday), though other nights can be just as busy at venues with 'ladies night' promotions. Dubai doesn't have a nightlife district as such: the best venues – most commonly in hotels or attached to sports and leisure facilities – are spread throughout the city.

Drinking venues divide into two types: the cheery British-style pubs which can be found in most large hotels, and smarter, more style-conscious bars often with live DJs later in the evening. Pubs generally open from noon to around 2am; bars tend to open later, at 6/7pm and stay open until as late as 3am.

Good pubs include the lively **Long's Bar** in the Towers Rotana hotel on Sheikh Zayed Road; the **Irish Village** at Dubai Tennis Stadium (www.theirishvillage.com), with outdoor seating in a pleasant garden; the convivial **Belgium Beer Café** at the Crowne Plaza in Festival City (www.belgianbeercafe.com); and the **Sherlock Holmes** pub in the Arabian Courtyard hotel near the Dubai Museum in Bur Dubai (www.sherlockholmespub.net).

It is Dubai's bars which really steal the show, however. High-rise bars with incredible views are a particular Dubai speciality. Notable venues include the classy **Alta Badia Bar**, on the 51st floor of the Jumeirah Emirates Towers Hotel; the **Skyview Bar** at the Burj Al Arab; and **Bar 44**, at the top of the Grosvenor House (www.bar44-dubai.com).

Waterfront bars are another big draw. The most memorable is probably **360°**, perched dramatically at the end of a break-water curling out to sea from the Jumeirah Beach Hotel, and offering unbeatable views of the Burj Al Arab and a very cool

Rooftop bar and wind-tower

ambience. **Sho Cho's** at the Dubai Marine Beach Resort and Spa in Jumeirah is another über-cool venue, popular with the city's beautiful people (www.sho-cho.com). Down in Dubai Marina, Le Meridien Mina Seyahi's open-air beach-side **Barasti Bar** is another perennially popular spot, with a refreshing lack of pretension (www.barasti beach.com).

Other places worth hunting out are the **Bahri Bar** at the Mina A'Salam hotel in Madinat Jumeirah, with Arabian styling and sublime Burj Al Arab views; the similarly styled **Rooftop Bar** at the One&Only Royal Mirage and the spectacular **Buddha Bar** at the Grosvenor House hotel (www.buddhabar.com).

There is also a clutch of decent wine bars in the city. The main venue is **The Agency**, with branches in the Emirates Towers Boulevard and Madinat Jumeirah.

Dubai has several good nightclubs, with guest DJs regularly flown in from Europe and elsewhere. One of the most popular is **Boracay Night** at the Asiana Hotel (www.boracayclub.com), while **N'Dulge** (tel: 04 426 0561) at the Atlantis resort on Palm Jumeirah is another attractive venue, with separate arena, lounge and terrace areas. Swankiest of all is the **Cavalli Club** (tel: 050 991 0400; http://dubai.cavalliclub.com) at the Fairmont Hotel, by the eponymous Italian designer – very posey and very bling. At the opposite end of the scale, the ever-popular **Zinc** (tel: 050 199 9271) at the

Crowne Plaza on Sheikh Zayed Road serves up attitude-free clubbing to an eclectic soundtrack.

Smaller venues worth hunting out include the chintzy little French-styled **Boudoir** (www.clubboudoirdubai.com) at Dubai Marine Beach Resort and Spa; and the Moroccan-themed **Kasbar** at the One&Only Royal Mirage.

CINEMA

Dubai has a number of modern, multi-screen cinemas attached to shopping malls. The offerings are mainly mainstream Hollywood movies, with few art-house pictures or regionally made films. The city has an IMAX screen at Ibn Battuta Mall. The showing of free double-bills at open-air venues in winter has become popular – try 'Movies Under The Stars' on the Wafi rooftop (October–May, Sundays from 8.30pm). The highlight of the year is the Dubai International Film Festival (https://dubai filmfest.com), which takes place at Madinat Jumeirah in December and attracts directors, producers and stars from Hollywood, Bollywood and the Middle East.

LIVE MUSIC

As well as attracting old favourites such as Elton John and Lionel Ritchie, Dubai dates are becoming more common on the world-tour schedules of contemporary chart toppers. For further information, check *Time Out*

Perks for women

Ladies Nights are a Dubai institution. These are usually held on Wednesday, Thursday or, most commonly, Tuesday nights in an attempt to drum up custom during the quieter midweek evenings, with lots of places around the city offering all sorts of deals for women, ranging from a couple of free cocktails up to complimentary champagne all night.

Dubai (www.timeoutdubai.com) or the monthly *What's On* (http://whatson.ae/dubai). Big-name acts usually perform at the **Dubai Media City Amphitheatre**; smaller concerts are held at the **Dubai Tennis Stadium** in Garhoud.

Jazz fans are catered to by the annual Dubai International Jazz Festival (January–February; www.dubaijazzfest.com); there is also regular jazz at **Up On The 10th** in the Radisson Blu hotel in Deira and the **Blue Bar**, at the Novotel off Sheikh Zayed Road.

PERFORMING ARTS

Dubai's first purpose-built theatre at **Madinat Jumeirah** (tel: 04 366 6546; https://madinatjumeirah.etixdubai.com) has been slow to develop a full season of entertainment. **Dubai Drama Group** has a permanent home in the Dubai Community Theatre and Arts Centre (tel: 04 341 4777; www.ductac.org) at Mall of the Emirates, which also hosts English-language touring productions. **The Laughter Factory** has been bringing British comedians to the city for several years (www.thelaughterfactory.com). For the latest information consult *Time Out Dubai* or *What's On* magazines.

DUBAI FOR CHILDREN

Most of the large shopping malls have dedicated children's entertainment zones/play areas. There are a number of child-centred attractions at the Dubai Mall including KidZania, where kids get to role-play various jobs, the hi-tech Sega Republic, and the Dubai Aquarium. Other kid-specific attractions include **Children's City** (www.childrencity.dm.gov.ae) and **Dubai Dolphinarium** (www.dubaidolphinarium.ae) in the Creek Park and **Stargate**, a space-themed entertainment complex in Zabeel Park.

Kids will also love **Wild Wadi** waterpark, **Ski Dubai**, and the attractions at the **Atlantis** resort.

CALENDAR OF EVENTS

January *Dubai Marathon* Leading long-distance runners come to Dubai. *Dubai 24 Hour* Classic motorsport endurance event at the Autodrome.

January–February *Dubai Shopping Festival* Shops across the city offer massive discounts and special promotions.

Dubai International Jazz Festival Performances by big-name jazz stars.

Dubai Desert Classic, Emirates Golf Course The Middle East's premier golfing tournament, attracting top international players.

February–March *Dubai Tennis Championships* Top male and female players battle it out at Dubai Tennis Stadium in Garhoud.

Taste of Dubai Food Festival, Dubai Media City Citywide foodie promotions, plus workshops with leading local and international chefs.

March *Dubai World Cup, Meydan racecourse* The world's richest horse race.

Art Dubai Huge international art fair.

SIKKA Art Fair alternative to Art Dubai, focusing on Arab artists.

Sharjah Biennial Art Festival (odd-numbered years only) Prestigious biennial art expo.

March–April *Abu Dhabi Desert Challenge* Rally drivers race in the desert.

April *Perrier Chill-Out Festival* Laidback music festival with top names.

August–September *Dubai Summer Surprises* Citywide retail promotions and mall-based entertainment.

October *Abu Dhabi Film Festival* Films from Arabia and beyond.

November *Abu Dhabi F1 Grand Prix, Yas Island.*

Dubai World Championship, Jumeirah Golf Estates Season-ending finale to the European Golf Tour.

ITF Al Habtoor Tennis Challenge, Dubai Marina.

December *UAE National Day (2 December)* Dhow races, parades, and traditional music and dance performances.

Dubai Ladies Masters, Emirates Golf Club Leading event on Ladies' European Tour.

Dubai Rugby Sevens, The Sevens Stadium Popular rugby tournament.

Dubai International Film Festival, Madinat Jumeirah Focusing on African, Asian and especially Arab cinema.

EATING OUT

You won't go hungry in Dubai – quite the opposite in fact, as the city continues to consolidate its position as the food capital of the Middle East. As you would expect, the city is a particularly good place to sample Arabian cuisine, but at the culinary crossroads between Europe, Asia and Arabia, it offers a cosmopolitan spread of cuisines, in a huge variety of settings. At the bottom of the scale, you can eat well for just a handful of dirhams at one of the city's streetside *shwarma* stands, inexpensive Lebanese cafés, or in one of the hundreds of bargain-basement curry houses that can be found throughout Bur Dubai and Karama. At the top of the scale, the sky's the limit, with opulent restaurants in spectacular waterfront or high-rise locations.

Standards at the best places are top-notch, and international celebrity chefs have also been drawn to the city – Gordon Ramsay, Gary Rhodes, Nobu Matsuhisa, Sanjeev Kapoor, Vineet Bhatia, Pierre Gagnaire and the late Santi Santamaria have all opened restaurants in the city (although Ramsay has now departed).

MEAL TIMES

Meals are eaten at the times you'd expect in any international city: breakfast from 6.30 to 9am, lunch between noon and 3pm and dinner not earlier than 8pm. That said, outside the hotels, many cafés and restaurants are open from breakfast to the early hours of the next morning.

The one time of year when the opening hours of cafés and restaurants vary from the norm is during Ramadan, when Muslims fast during the day for a month. Throughout this period, which moves from year to year, even non-Muslims are forbidden to eat, drink or smoke in public between sunrise and sunset. Accordingly, non-hotel restaurants are closed until sunset, though some may keep their kitchens open to serve take-away meals. During the day, it is possible to eat in hotel restaurants that are shielded from view behind wooden screens, but alcohol won't be served until the evening.

WHERE TO EAT

If you want to drink alcohol with your meal, your eating options are immediately restricted to licensed restaurants in hotels – although don't assume that just because a place is unlicensed the food will be below par. Wherever you're going, the best places can get booked up quickly, particularly at weekends; so it pays to reserve.

Al Muntaha restaurant in the Burj al Arab

Hotels

There is a vast range of different places to eat in the city's myriad hotels, ranging from functional 24-hour coffee shops and buffet restaurants through to ultra-swanky fine-dining palaces. The majority of hotel restaurants are licensed, although there are exceptions. Many of the best places take advantage of their spectacular locations. These include a number of magical beachfront restaurants (such as Pierchic at Al Qasr hotel, or Eauzone at the One&Only Royal Mirage), plus various places in spectacular high-rise locations at (or near) the top of the city's skyscrapers (Al Muntaha in the Burj al Arab and At.Mosphere in the Burj Khalifa are probably the three best known). Other places take advantage of waterside locations around the city (Thai Kitchen at the Park Hyatt, overlooking the Creek, for example, or Thiptara at The Palace hotel, which overlooks the Dubai Fountain).

For something with a more local flavour, Dubai's hotels are a good place to sample traditional Arabian fare, often with live music and belly-dancing – these places frequently don't get going till late, but stay lively into the small hours. Al Tannour at the Crowne Plaza in Sheikh Zayed Road and Al Qasr at the Dubai Marine Beach Resort are two good spots.

On the street

For a quintessential Dubai meal, nothing beats a simple *shwarma*, bought at a local café or pavement *shwarma* stand and eaten at a streetside table watching the crowds go by – a simple, tasty meal for little more than a dollar or two. Slightly more elaborate (but still inexpensive) Arabian food can be found at numerous cafés across the city, most of which will also do a good line in shisha. Good areas for inexpensive Arabian food include the Creekside in the old city centre (Kanzaman in Shindagha is popular), Sheikh Zayed Road, and Al Diyafah Street in the suburb of Satwa (with Beirut and Al Mallah the two best-known places). The Gulf-wide chain of Automatic restaurants can also be found across the city,

Friday brunch

The Dubai Friday brunch is a city institution, equivalent to the British Sunday roast. It is particularly popular among the city's European expat set, while many restaurants lay on all-you-can-eat (and sometimes drink, as well) deals. Brunch usually kicks off around midday, and can last for the remainder of the afternoon. Check *Time Out Dubai* for all the latest venues and deals.

offering substantial and very reasonably priced Lebanese cuisine; the local Japengo chain (also with branches citywide) also does good Lebanese as part of its wide-ranging menu. Look out too for branches of the Zaatar w Zeit chain, which offers good Lebanese-style fast food at bargain prices (www.zaatarwzeit.net).

Shish kebab skewers

Cheap but well-prepared food can also be found at the innumerable inexpensive Indian and Pakistani cafés dotted across the city. The majority of these can be found in Bur Dubai and in the 'curry corridor' stretching along Sheikh Zayed Road from just past the BurJuman Centre up to Karama. Cafés tend to specialise either in generic North Indian/Pakistani-style meat curries, or in vegetarian cuisine (the international Saravanna Bhavan chain has a number of branches in the city and is particularly good for both North and South Indian vegetarian cooking, www.saravanabhavan.com).

Café society

Dubai has its own distinctive café culture – hanging out over coffee and a shisha plays a central role in Arabian culture. Most of the best places have a decidedly local flavour, patronised by Emiratis and expat Arabs and usually with a good shisha selection. More European-style cafés include the popular Lime Tree Café in Jumeirah (www.thelimetreecafe.com), the XVA Café in Bastakiya

Enjoying a dinner cruise on Dubai Creek

(www.xvahotel.com/cafe), the funky Dutch-owned More in Al Murooj, the DIFC and the Mall of the Emirates (www.more-cafe.com), and the chintzy Shakespeare and Co., with several branches around the city (www.shakespeare-and-co.com).

Malls and sports clubs

All malls have food courts offering the usual international fast food and chain restaurants, but look out for appealing venues that are located away from the food courts. At Wafi there is the arty European Elements Café (www.elements-cafe.com) and the Lebanese deli and restaurant, Wafi Gourmet (www.wafigourmet.com). At Mercato in Jumeirah and the BurJuman Centre in Bur Dubai, there is the French-style Paul boulangerie and café (www.paul-bakeries.com). The classy Australian café chain Dôme has outlets at BurJuman, Jumeirah Plaza and Souk Madinat Jumeirah (www.domeuae.com). An alternative to the American and European coffee franchises in Jumeirah is Gerard in Magrudy's Mall, a Dubai institution. Almaz by Momo, at Mall of the Emirates, is worth a visit for its sumptuous North African cuisine.

The city's sports clubs also provide a home for a number of perennially popular restaurants. The various Creekside venues (with stunning views) at the Dubai Creek Golf and Yacht Club continue to attract a local clientele, while the nearby Aviation Club in Garhoud is home to another lively cluster of restaurants. Further south, the sparkling Dubai Marina Yacht Club, overlooking the Marina, has an appealing selection of places to eat and drink.

Dinner cruises

For a meal with a difference, try one of the dinner cruises on the Creek aboard a traditional wooden dhow. These are offered by pretty much every tour operator in the city and are usually most easily arranged through your hotel. Cruise operators include Rikks Cruises (tel: 04 458 6664, www.rikks.net), which offers some of the cheapest cruises in town, and the more upmarket Al Mansour Dhow, a dinner cruise operated by the Radisson Blu hotel (tel: 04 222 7171).

For a modern alternative to the traditional dhow, Bateaux Dubai (tel: 04 814 5553, www.jaresortshotels.com/bateaux-dubai) runs cruises in its state-of-the-art glass-sided boat, offering a touch more luxury than other operators, plus better-than-average food. Alternatively, Danat Dubai Cruises (tel: 04 351 1117) run upmarket cruises along the Creek and also out along the coast, aboard their state-of-the-art catamaran.

WHAT TO EAT

Though it is not widely available, Emirati food consists of simple rice, fish or meat dishes, such as *matchbous* (spiced lamb with rice), *hareis* (slow-cooked wheat and lamb) and *fareed* (a meat and vegetable stew poured over thin bread). Sadly Emirati food hardly ever appears on restaurant menus – the best place to try it is usually the Khan Murjan Restaurant in the Khan Murjan Souk.

Traditional Arabian food (often described as 'Lebanese', since many of the most common dishes come from Lebanon) features a spread of hot and/or cold *mezze* (small dishes, like a kind of Middle Eastern tapas) followed by grilled main courses – such as lamb or chicken *shwarma* sliced from a vertical spit, or mixed grills and locally caught fish – served with Arabic bread, French fries or rice. The best places serve up a considerable variety of *mezze,* including hot dishes such as *kibbeh* (fried minced lamb with crushed wheat), *sambousek* (samosa-style pastries filled with minced lamb and pine nuts or *haloumi* cheese or spinach), and *arayes* (bread stuffed with minced lamb, tomato and cheese). Cold *mezze* includes hummus, *moutabbal* (a paste of grilled aubergine with *tahini* and lemon), *tabouleh* (a finely chopped parsley salad with mint, fresh tomatoes, onion and crushed wheat, topped with olive oil and lemon), and *fattoush* (a green salad with toasted bread).

⊙ SHISHA PIPES

Shisha smoking is a very popular way to round off a meal in many Arabic restaurants. Shisha are free-standing water pipes consisting of a water-filled container topped with tobacco, a small bowl of glowing charcoal and a long pipe with a mouthpiece. It has been nicknamed 'hubble-bubble' in English because of the bubbling sound the water makes as the smoke is drawn through the pipe, but is also known as 'hookah', after *huqqah*, the Arabic word for container, and *nargileh*, which is derived from the Persian word for coconut, *nargil* (coconuts were once used to contain the water).

Shisha can be smoked plain but is usually offered in a range of flavours – anything from apple, strawberry or melon through to fruit cocktail or cappuccino. Aficionados claim that because the smoke is drawn through water it is cleansed of much of its nicotine content. Even so, shisha can be habit-forming, although if you only sample it once or twice you're unlikely to become hooked on the hookah.

Arabic desserts include *kashta* (clotted cream topped with pistachio, pine nuts and honey); and *Umm Ali* (literally, 'Mother of Ali'), a bread and butter pudding with sultanas and coconut, topped with nuts.

Arabic or Lebanese 'fast food' comprises sandwiches made with Arabic bread and a variety of fillings, including *shwarma* or falafel (mashed chickpeas and spices deep fried in flattened balls), served

Baba Ghanoush and Fatayer Bil Sabanikh as part of a mezze

with a salad garnish. Also worth sampling is *manakeesh*, a round, pizza-like bread covered with *zatar*, a mixture of dried thyme, sesame seed, spices and olive oil.

Though the Muslim population is forbidden to eat pork or consume alcohol, both are used as ingredients on hotel menus and are flagged up for those who must abstain. Without exception, all other meat is halal. Non-hotel venues substitute beef, bacon or chicken sausages for pork.

WHAT TO DRINK

Popular beverages throughout the Gulf are *shai* (tea) and *kahwa* (coffee). Traditional Arabian coffee is quite unlike that found in the West; it is served very strong, flavoured with cardamom and other spices, and served in little cups without handles. Tea is widely available, including Indian-style *masala chai*. A fantastic selection of fresh juices is available in Arabic restaurants and at juice stalls.

TO HELP YOU ORDER...

English is widely spoken, so English speakers should not
have a problem, particularly in hotels. Arabic-speaking
service staff, mostly from the Levant or North Africa,
will understand some English, but here are a few Arabic
phrases, just in case:

Do you have a table? **Indaakum towla?**

Is there anyone here who speaks English? **Haal yoojad
ahad yatakaalam al-lugha al-ingleezia?**

May I see the menu, please? **Laow samaht, ana ureed
laeehat ataamm?**

Excuse me. **Afwan.**

I don't eat meat. **La akul lahem.**

What do you recommend? **Maatha tansah?**

May I have the bill, please? **Fatoura, laow samaht.**

I'd like ... **Ana ureed...**

thank you **shukran**	I've finished. **Ana khallast.**
yes **nam**	no **la**
beef **lahem bakar**	milk **haleeb**
bread **khobez**	pepper **bahar**
chicken **dajaj**	rice **rouz**
coffee **kahwa**	salad **salata**
dessert **helou**	salt **melh**
fish **samak**	sandwich **sandweesh**
French fries **batata makleea**	soup **shorba**
fruit **fawakah**	tea **shai**
ice cream **booza**	vegetables **khodra**
lamb **lahem harouf**	water **mai**

... AND READ THE MENU

bajella local variation on boiled foul

esh asaraya cheesecake with cream topping

Lebanese kibbeh, a croquette stuffed with minced beef or lamb

foul fava-bean stew with garlic and lemon

ghuzi whole roast lamb with rice and pine nuts

hallaweeyat desserts

jarjir rocket leaves and onion

kofta minced lamb with parsley and onion

lahem meat (not including chicken)

logaimat fried balls made from egg, flour and saffron

mashawee grills

mehalabiya milk custard with pistachios and rosewater

roub cucumber with yoghurt

salatat zatar thyme salad with onions, lemon and olive oil

shish kebab grilled mutton marinated with cumin and cinnamon

shish tawouq grilled chicken pieces marinated with cumin and cinnamon

toum crushed garlic and mayonnaise

PLACES TO EAT

The price categories below are based on the average cost of a meal for two with a glass of wine each in hotel venues, or soft drinks elsewhere.

$$$$$	More than Dhs500
$$$$	Dhs400–500
$$$	Dhs200–400
$$	Dhs100–200
$	Less than Dhs100

DUBAI

The coast

Al Mahara $$$$$ *Burj Al Arab, Umm Suqeim, tel: 04 301 7600.* Centred on an enormous fish tank, this subterranean seafood restaurant is one of Dubai's most expensive. Men are expected to wear a jacket at dinner; no jeans. Open daily 12.30–3.30pm and 7–11.30pm.

Amala $$$$ *Jumeirah Zabeel Saray, The Palm Jumeirah, tel: 04 453 0444.* Indian fine-dining restaurant in the Jumeirah Zabeel Saray hotel, this place has had rave reviews for its opulent décor and superb classical North Indian cooking – and the tasting menu at Dhs325 is a good deal. Open daily 6pm–midnight, Fri–Sat also lunch 1–4pm.

Buddha Bar $$$$ *Grosvenor House, Al Sufouh Road, tel: 04 317 6000,* www.buddhabar-dubai.com. One of the best-looking restaurants in Dubai, with a fine array of Japanese, Thai and Chinese mains. Open daily 7pm–1am, Thu–Fri until 2am.

Indego by Vineet $$$$ *Grosvenor House, Al Sufouh Road, tel: 04 317 6000.* Overseen by Vineet Bhatia, India's first Michelin-starred chef, this stylish restaurant showcases Bhatia's outstanding 'contemporary Indian' cooking, with international ingredients and techniques. Open daily 7pm–midnight.

Japengo $$ *Mall of the Emirates, Sheikh Zayed Road, tel: 04 341 1671.* Chic café-restaurant, with an eclectic menu featuring everything from sushi and sashimi to stir-fries, pizzas, pastas, *mezze* and lamb chops, plus sandwiches and salads. There are other branches, including one overlooking the canal in the Souk Madinat Jumeirah, the other in Mirdif City Centre and the DIFC district. Times vary depending on location.

Lime Tree Café $$ *Jumeirah Road, tel: 04 325 6325,* www.thelimetreecafe. com. Set in an attractive modern villa, this neat café offers a classic slice of expat Jumeirah life. Healthy specialities include tasty wraps, delicious smoothies and the best carrot cake in Dubai. Open daily 7.30am–6pm.

Nina $$$$ *Arabian Courtyard, One&Only Royal Mirage, tel: 04 399 9999.* Innovative modern Indian restaurant, combining subcontinental flavours with international ingredients and cooking techniques – anything from traditional butter chicken through to frogs' legs and *rambutan*. Open Mon–Sat 7–11.30pm.

Pai Tai $$$$ *Al Qasr hotel, Madinat Jumeirah, tel: 04 432 3232.* One of the city's most romantic places to eat, with live music and stunning views of the Burj Al Arab from the candlelit terrace. The menu features Thai classics, including spicy salads and meat and seafood curries. Open Sun–Thu 6–11.30pm, Fri–Sat 12.30–3pm, 6.30–11.30pm.

Pierchic $$$$$ *Al Qasr hotel, Madinat Jumeirah, tel: 04 366 6705.* A fabulous seafood venue at the end of a wooden pier with views of the Madinat Jumeirah resort and Burj Al Arab. Open daily 12.30–3pm and 6–11pm.

Rhodes W1 $$$$$ *Grosvenor House Hotel, tel: 04 317 6000,* www.rw1-dubai.com. Dubai outpost of UK celebrity chef Gary Rhodes, with a short but inventive menu showcasing modern European cuisine, accompanied by classic British puddings like jam roly-poly and steamed steak and kidney pudding. Open Mon–Sat 7–11.30pm.

Tagine $$$ *One&Only Royal Mirage, Al Sufouh Road, tel: 04 399 9999.* Exquisitely decorated little Moroccan restaurant with Arabian Nights décor and a fine array of traditional Moroccan cuisine, including tagines and traditional dishes like spicy harira soup, lamb's brain and pigeon pie. Open daily 7–11.30pm.

Zheng He's $$$$ *Mina A'Salam, Madinat Jumeirah, tel: 04 432 3232.* One of the top Chinese restaurants in Dubai, with sumptuous décor and superb classic and contemporary Chinese fare, including excellent dim sum. Open daily for lunch noon–2.30pm and for dinner 6.30–11pm.

Sheikh Zayed Road

Almaz by Momo $$$ *Harvey Nichols, Mall of the Emirates, Sheikh Zayed Road, tel: 04 409 8877.* Dubai version of the celebrity hang-out in London, offering mezze and traditional Moroccan mains in a contemporary North African-themed interior. Open Thu–Sat 10am–midnight, Sun–Wed 10am–10pm.

Al Nafoorah $$$ *Jumeirah Emirates Towers, tel: 04 319 8760.* The best Lebanese restaurant in town, with beautifully prepared hot and cold mezze, grills and a good wine list, including Lebanese vintages. Open daily noon–3.30pm and 6–11.30pm.

Alta Badia $$$$ *Jumeirah Emirates Towers Hotel, Sheikh Zayed Road, tel: 04 319 8771.* An Italian restaurant at Jumeirah Emirates Towers, serving a mix of classic Italian flavours and chef's creative culinary inventions with a wide selection of vegetarian dishes available, all amplified by great views. Lunch Sun–Thu noon–3pm, dinner Sun–Sat 6pm–midnight.

Armani/Amal $$$$$ *Armani Hotel, Downtown Dubai, tel: 04 888 3666.* Old-time traditional Indian favourites, including tasty curries and tandoori. A great dining experience, and though a bit pricey, it includes spectacular views of the Dubai Fountain (ask for terrace seating). Open daily 7–11pm.

At.Mosphere $$$$$ *Burj Khalifa, Downtown Dubai, tel: 04 888 3828,* www. atmosphereburjkhalifa.com. At.mosphere is the world's highest bar and restaurant, located on the 122nd floor of the soaring Burj Khalifa, the world's tallest building. Choose either the lounge for a drink, light meal or pricey afternoon tea or the restaurant which offers upmarket fare in an elegant dining room.

The Exchange Grill $$$$$ *Fairmont Hotel, Sheikh Zayed Road, tel: 04 311 8559.* The city's most exclusive steakhouse, this small and very upmarket establishment serves choice Gold Angus and Stockyard Wagyu cuts, accompanied by one of the city's most extensive wine lists. Open daily 7pm–midnight.

The Noodle House $$ *Jumeirah Emirates Towers, tel: 04 319 8088,* www.thenoodlehouse.com. Popular Asian fusion chain restaurant with bench and table seating that is crowded with office workers at lunchtimes. Other locations within the city include Souk Madinat Jumeirah and the Dubai Mall. Open daily noon–midnight.

Teatro $$$ *Towers Rotana, Sheikh Zayed Road, tel: 04 312 2202.* Serving five different cuisines (Thai, Chinese, Japanese sushi, Indian and Italian), this lively restaurant has a theatrical theme without pretensions. Open daily 6pm–2am.

Thiptara $$$$$ *The Palace – Downtown Dubai, Emaar Boulevard, Downtown Burj Dubai, tel: 04 888 3444.* This beautiful Thai restaurant is set in a traditional wooden pavilion jutting out into the waters of the lake behind the Dubai Mall, with peerless views of the Burj Khalifa and Dubai Fountain. The menu concentrates on sumptuous Bangkok-style seafood, plus meat and vegetarian options. Open daily 6–11.30pm.

Zuma $$$$ *The Gate Village 06, DIFC, tel: 04 425 5660,* www.zumarestaurant.com. This über-chic bar-restaurant is a hit both with Dubai's fashionistas and local foodies, thanks to its cool ambience and excellent range of classic and contemporary Japanese fare. Sat–Wed noon–1am, Thu–Fri until 2am.

Bur Dubai

Bastakiah Nights $$$ *Bastakiya, tel: 04 353 7772.* Good Arabic and Iranian food served in a wonderful traditional wind-towered house. Open daily 12.30–3pm and 6.30–11.30pm.

Chhappan Bhog $ *Sheikh Khalifa Bin Zayed Road (Trade Centre Road), Karama, tel: 04 396 8176.* A friendly Indian restaurant specialising in vegetarian *thalis* (platters made up of various dishes). Open daily 9am–midnight.

Ravi's $ *Near Satwa Roundabout, tel: 04 331 5353.* This legendary little café remains popular with locals, expats and tourists alike for its cheap and tasty Pakistani-style chicken, mutton and vegetable curries, while the outdoor seating offers a good (if noisy) perch from which to enjoy the passing street life. Open daily 5pm–3am.

Deira

Asha's $$$ *Wafi, Oud Metha, tel: 04 324 4100.* Owned by legendary Bollywood chanteuse Asha Bhosle, this smart Wafi restaurant offers Indian classics alongside more unusual regional specialities, including recipes from Asha's own cookbook. Open daily 12.30–3.30pm and 7pm–midnight.

Ashiana by Vineet $$$$ *Sheraton Dubai Creek Hotel, Baniyas Road, tel: 04 228 1111, www.ashianadubai.com.* One of Dubai's oldest upmarket Indian restaurants specialising in hearty North Indian cuisine with rich and flavoursome sauces. Michelin-starred chef Vineet Bhatia manages the menu. Daily lunch noon–3pm, dinner 7–11pm.

The Boardwalk $$$ *Dubai Creek Golf and Yacht Club, tel: 04 205 4647.* The mainstream menu of international food is tasty enough, but it is the terrific views from the outdoor seating on the restaurant's boardwalk that steal the show. Open Sun–Thu noon–midnight, Fri and Sat 8am–midnight.

More $$ *D71, near Financial Centre Road, Al Murooj, tel: 04 343 3779, www.more-cafe.co.* A funky Dutch-owned bistro with a wide range of superior international café fare. Difficult to beat for its combination of excellent atmosphere, value and service. There are also branches in the Mall of the Emirates and DIFC. Open daily 7.30am–11pm.

Shabestan $$$$ *Radisson Blu, Baniyas Road, tel: 04 205 7333.* Perhaps the best Iranian restaurant in the city, specialising in huge *chelo* kebabs, fish stews and other Persian specialities, accompanied by an Iranian band of violin, drum and santour (nightly except Sat). Open daily 12.30–3.30pm and 7.30–11.30pm.

Table 9 $$$$ *Hilton Dubai Creek, Baniyas Road, tel: 04 212 7551, www3. hilton.com*. Formerly Gordon Ramsay's Verre, this outstanding restaurant offers the same top-notch modern European fine-dining as before, but with a more flexible menu, relaxed ambience and lower prices. Sun–Fri 6.30–11pm.

The Thai Kitchen $$$$ *Park Hyatt, Garhoud, tel: 04 602 1814*, www.hyatt restaurants.com. One of the best Thai restaurants in town, set on the Park Hyatt's idyllic Creekside terrace, it offers a sumptuous range of unusual regional specialities. Open daily 7pm–midnight, also Friday brunch 12.30–4pm.

A–Z TRAVEL TIPS

A SUMMARY OF PRACTICAL INFORMATION

A

ACCOMMODATION

There's a huge range of accommodation in Dubai, including innumerable five-star hotels, although good accommodation lower down the price scale is more difficult to find. The cheapest accommodation is the one- and two-star hotels around the old city centre in Bur Dubai and Deira, although even here you'll struggle to find a room for less than US$75 a night. Rates at the city's more upmarket hotels start at around US$150 a night, rising to as much as US$2000 a night. For beach hotels it pays to reserve as far ahead as possible.

Dubai's high season runs roughly from October through to April. The low season stretches through the hotter months of May to August, during which prices can fall significantly.

ADMISSION CHARGES

Admission charges to government-run heritage sites, museum and parks are extremely modest, sometimes free, and never more than Dhs5. Conversely, entrance fees to privately run attractions can be stratospheric, particularly for families, with prices pushing north of US$100 for two adults and two children.

AIRPORTS

Dubai International Airport, otherwise known as DXB (tel: 04 224 5555, www.dubaiairports.ae), is centrally located on the Deira side of Dubai Creek, in Garhoud and Al Qusais districts. There are three terminals. Terminal 3 is where all Emirates flights arrive and depart. Terminal 1 handles other long-haul international flights, while Terminal 2 handles short-haul flights. Both Terminals 1 and 3 have their own dedicated metro stations, and there are plentiful taxis, although note that these charge a Dhs 20 surcharge when picking up from the airport.

Since 2013, visitors to Dubai have also had the option of **Al Maktoum International Airport**, known as DWC, located at the heart of the Dubai

World Central development (www.dubaiairports.ae), south of the city.

ALCOHOL

Dubai has a relatively liberal attitude to the consumption of alcohol by non-Muslims as long as it is limited to licensed premises and people do not drink and drive. Beers, wines and spirits are readily available in hotels (rooms, restaurants and bars) and clubs, but not, generally, anywhere else. Alcohol is not sold in supermarkets and only residents with government-issued liquor licences can buy from licensed vendors MMI and A&E.

Dubai has a zero-tolerance approach to drink-driving and offenders face a lengthy legal process, three weeks in prison and even deportation, whatever the amount of alcohol detected in the blood. Note that you risk arrest if driving the morning after a heavy night if there is still any trace of alcohol in your system. Being drunk and disorderly in public is also an offence, as is buying alcohol for a Muslim. The sale of alcohol everywhere is restricted during the Islamic holy month of Ramadan.

B

BUDGETING FOR YOUR TRIP

Shop around for the best deals on flights and accommodation as there are lots of good value packages available. Dubai is an expensive place for visitors, though eating out (in cheaper restaurants) and travelling around using public transport needn't be too costly.

Travelling to Dubai. Combination airfare–hotel deals are often cheaper than separately arranged air travel and accommodation. The best prices are low season (May–Sept), but that's the hottest time of the year in the UAE.

Accommodation. If you are not on a package deal, the cost for a standard double room ranges from around Dhs300–350 per night in a one-star hotel up to around Dhs750 at the cheapest five-star hotel through to around Dhs16,000 per night for a suite at the seven-star Burj Al Arab.

Meals and drinks. It's possible to eat for as little as Dhs15 per person if you go for a *shwarma* sandwich in a street-side café or a curry in a no-nonsense Indian or Pakistani outlet. Main courses in most decent Western-style, non-hotel restaurants are Dhs25–50. For fine dining, budget for upwards of Dhs70 per person for main courses. Cans of soft drinks start at Dhs2 in shops, but are marked up by as much as 800 percent in restaurants. Freshly made juices cost Dhs6–15. Imported alcoholic drinks are generally the same price or more expensive than they would be in the West.

Local transport. Transport is cheap if you stick to public transport: tickets on the Dubai Metro and buses start from Dhs3, while the trip across the Creek by *abra* (water taxi) costs just Dhs1. Taxis are reasonably priced, too, with a minimum charge of Dhs10 and a cost of around Dhs2.4 per kilometre (although taxis picked up at the airport have a Dhs20 surcharge). A taxi from the Dubai International Airport to Deira or Bur Dubai will cost around Dhs40–50; considerably more (Dhs80–100) to the more distant resort hotels along the Jumeirah coast. Many hotels offer a free airport transfer service. The ordinary fare for taxis between the resort hotels and the city centre is around Dhs80–100 one way, so consider taking the shuttle buses provided by most hotels.

A half-day desert safari with a tour company costs around Dhs250–350. The price of petrol is around Dhs10 per imperial gallon for unleaded Special (95 octane).

C

CAR HIRE

Hiring a car is one of the best ways to explore the city of Dubai. Car-hire companies include **Avis** (www.avis.ae), **Budget** (www.budget-uae.com), **Thrifty** (www.thriftyuae.com), **Europcar** (www.europcardubai.com), **Hertz** (www.hertz.ae) and **Sixt** (www.sixt.ae), with numerous offices citywide – see the websites for details of office locations. The cheapest cars start from under Dhs150 a day, including insurance and unlimited mileage.

Most national driving licences are recognised, but it's a good idea to have a valid international driving licence with you as back-up in case the rules change. For insurance reasons, visitors can only drive rental cars and not privately owned vehicles. To drive a resident friend's car, for example, visitors must get a temporary licence from Dubai Police.

CHILDREN

Childcare facilities are on a par with those in the West. Most malls have changing facilities in the women's public toilets; many also have supervised indoor play areas. Many of the more upmarket beach resorts have kids' club and babysitting services.

CLIMATE

Dubai is an arid, desert nation with mild, pleasant winters and very hot, humid summers. While the country enjoys year-round sunshine, the reality is that you can't be out in the sun for long periods in the summer. The period from May to September is particularly hot, with temperatures topping 48°C (118°F) during the day, with around 90 percent humidity.

From October to April, however, the weather is glorious, with monthly averages between 22°C (71°F) and 32°C (90°F), and lows of 10°C (50°F) (evenings can be quite chilly). Humidity also falls considerably at this time of year. Weather-wise, this is undoubtedly the best time to visit, but commensurate with the fall in temperatures is a rise in accommodation costs. What rain there is (about 87mm (3.4inches) per year) tends to fall on isolated days between October and March, when heavy morning fog can also occur.

CLOTHING

While swimming trunks and bikinis are fine at the beach (though going topless is not an option anywhere), they are not acceptable in other public areas, such as residential neighbourhoods near beaches, or in souks and malls. It's fine to expose arms and legs, and it's increasingly acceptable for women to bare their shoulders, but shorts and skirts shouldn't ride too high. Generally, men and women are expected to dress modestly, particularly during the Muslim holy month of Ramadan.

Dubai is hot in summer and warm in winter, so lightweight cottons and linens are advisable. Winter evenings can be surprisingly cool, so pack a cardigan or jumper, particularly if you want to enjoy an alfresco evening meal.

CRIME AND SAFETY

Crime is relatively rare in Dubai. Generally, visitors won't encounter criminal activity and need not be concerned about being extra cautious with their possessions. Most people feel safe on the city streets even late at night. Certainly, there are no neighbourhoods to avoid or gangs of rabble-rousing youths to steer clear of. However, follow your usual precautions and make sure you get comprehensive travel and medical insurance before travelling.

You are actually much more likely to fall foul of the law yourself in Dubai than to be the victim of crime – a recent study showed that British nationals were more likely to be arrested in the UAE than in any other country in the world. The range of possible offences includes possession of drugs (even microscopic quantities, or in one's bloodstream on arrival) and traffic-related offences (drink-driving particularly), through to apparently harmless actions such as kissing in public or gesturing at fellow motorists who have annoyed you. Note that many drugs available over the counter or on prescription in the West are illegal in Dubai. Homosexuality is also illegal, although prosecution of Westerners is extremely rare.

The US-led 'war on terror' has led to increased concerns for the safety of citizens of countries associated with American military activity in the region. The UAE is no exception and vigilance against terrorism is recommended.

Call Dubai Police's **Department for Tourist Security** on 800 4438 (www.dubaipolice.gov.ae).

CUSTOMS AND ENTRY REQUIREMENTS

Non-renewable 30-day visas are available free on arrival at the airport for visitors from 19 countries including the UK, Ireland, the United States, Canada, Australia, New Zealand, and several European and selected Asian countries. For details of longer visas, see www.visitdubai.com. Those who don't qualify for a visa on arrival, including South African citizens, can get a 30-day, paid non-renewable tourist visa through a hotel or tour operator sponsor. This should be arranged before entry to the UAE: visitors should ensure they have a fax copy of the visa with them and they should stop to collect the original at a designated desk in the airport before they reach passport control.

The duty-free allowance for arrivals in Dubai is four litres of alcohol (or 12 cans of beer), 400 cigarettes or 0.5kg of tobacco. A licence is required to drink or transport alcohol in Dubai, however no one checks tourists at the airport.

For more information on Dubai customs visit www.dubaicustoms.gov.ae.

D

DRIVING (See also Car hire)

Traffic drives on the right-hand side of the road inthe UAE, so vehicles are left-hand drive. The speed limits on most city streets are 60–80kph (37–50mph), and 100–120kph (62–75mph) on main highways. On road signs, distances are indicated in kilometres.

The road system in the UAE is good, but the general standard of driving can be impatient and aggressive. Accidents are common and the UAE has one of the highest traffic-accident death rates in the world. Lane discipline is poor, so on roads with more than a single lane in one direction, drivers should be aware of what's happening behind and on either side of them before manoeuvring. The fact that major arteries are under radar surveillance seems not to deter high-speed driving. Also bear in mind that around the city, taxi drivers have a nasty habit of swerving, stopping suddenly and blocking traffic if they spot a fare at the roadside, so keep a safe distance.

Outside Dubai, particularly on the Hatta highway, there's a possibility of camels wandering onto roads, so be cautious, particularly at night.

Seat belts are compulsory for drivers and front-seat passengers in the UAE. Children under 10 are not allowed to sit in the front passenger seat.

In the city, parking is in designated paid parking zones – look for the orange signs and solar-powered meters. Fees start from Dhs2 per hour. You can pay in coins, with a prepaid card, NOL card, or an Emirati mobile phone (for more information see www.mpark.rta.ae). The fine for not displaying a valid ticket starts at Dhs100. Speeding fines start from Dhs400. Sheikh Zayed Road between Garhoud Bridge and Interchange 4 is a toll road, as is Maktoum Bridge and the Airport Road. There are no toll booths, you will need to use a pre-paid Salik Card (Dhs100). Each time you pass a toll gate, Dhs4 will be deducted from the card. For more information visit www.salik.gov.ae. If you are involved in a road accident, stop and wait for the police. A police report on every level of accident is required for insurance claims. If you are stopped by the police at any time, you must be able to produce your driving licence and car hire/insurance papers (originals, not copies) there and then.

Unless you are an experienced off-road driver you should not consider hiring a four-wheel drive to head into the harsh and difficult terrain of the desert outside Dubai.

E

ELECTRICITY
The mains electricity in Dubai is 220/240 volts and 50 cycles. Wall sockets are designed for British-type, 13-amp three-pin plugs. Adaptors for two-pin appliances are available in supermarkets.

EMBASSIES AND CONSULATES
As Abu Dhabi, not Dubai, is the federal capital of the UAE, Dubai tends to have foreign consulates, rather than embassies. The telephone numbers for selected countries are:

Australia: 04 508 7100
Canada: 04 404 8444
Ireland: 02 495 8200 (Abu Dhabi)
New Zealand: 04 270 0100

South Africa: 04 397 5222
United Kingdom: 04 309 4444
United States: 04 309 4000

EMERGENCIES

Dial 999 for police or ambulance, or 997 for fire. Non-emergency inquiries can be made on 901.

ETIQUETTE

Although the UAE is a very liberal country compared with other states in the Gulf region, it is still a conservative Muslim country and visitors should respect this. Women especially should remember that clothing that is acceptable in a nightclub or on a beach is not appropriate to wear on the street during the day.

Outside the cities, dress more conservatively. Everyone should cover their upper arms and women should wear longer skirts or trousers. Men should not wear shorts in a business situation.

If visiting the home of a UAE citizen it is customary to remove shoes before venturing on to the carpets. Avoid showing the soles of your feet when sitting down. If you wish to take a present, a box of pastries or sweetmeats is a safe option.

During the holy month of Ramadan do not eat, smoke or drink in public.

G

GETTING THERE

Most visitors arrive at Dubai International Airport, though cruise ships dock at Dubai Cruise Terminal in Port Rashid. Alternatively, it is possible to fly into the neighbouring emirates of Abu Dhabi and Sharjah and cross into Dubai by road.

Dubai's International Airport (www.dubaiairports.ae) is the major Gulf hub for international air travel, with numerous connections worldwide. There are currently nonstop flights to Dubai from London with Emirates,

British Airways, Virgin and Royal Brunei Airlines, and numerous one-stop options with several European and Asian carriers and also with Etihad, Qatar Airways and Gulf Air. Emirates also fly nonstop to Dubai from a number of regional UK airports. From the US, there are a few nonstop flights with Emirates, plus one-stop options with a range of other North American carriers. Al Maktoum International Airport opened for passenger services in 2013, but this is a way off competing for the title of Dubai's most significant international airport.

The flying time from London to Dubai, direct, is about seven hours.

GUIDES AND TOURS (see also Tourist information)

Half-day **city sightseeing tours** organised by tour companies combine the main heritage sights with the city's striking modern architecture. An alternative is a hop-on, hop-off ticket with the Big Bus Company (tel: 04 340 7709, www.bigbustours.com), which operates open-top, double-decker buses daily on city and beach routes. To view Dubai from both the highway and the Creek, take the amphibious Wonder Bus, operated by Wonder Bus Tours (tel: 04 359 5656, www.wonderbusdubai.net), which departs three times daily from the BurJuman Centre in Bur Dubai.

The Sheikh Mohammed Centre for Cultural Understanding (tel: 04 353 6666, www.cultures.ae) runs **walking tours** of Al Fahidi Historic District at 10.30am on Tuesdays, Thursdays and Sundays and at 9am on Saturdays, and tours of Jumeirah Mosque Saturday through Thursday, beginning at 10am. The centre also organises visits to the homes of Emirati families.

Other tours include **desert safaris** and other desert trips, dhow cruises and tours of neighbouring emirates, as well as other activities, from fishing trips to helicopter rides. The leading local tour company is Arabian Adventures, a subsidiary of Emirates airline (tel: 04 272 2426, www. arabian-adventures.com). Other reliable operators include Alpha Tours (tel: 04 701 9111, www.alphatoursdubai.com), Net Tours (tel: 04 425 4450) and Orient Tours (tel: 04 282 8238, www.orient-tours-uae.com).

For details of dhow tours and trips by helicopter or hot-air balloon, see page 85.

H

HEALTH AND MEDICAL CARE

The number to dial for an ambulance is 998. There are good government hospitals as well as numerous private clinics. The main emergency hospital is the government-run Rashid Hospital (tel: 04 219 2000) near Maktoum Bridge in Bur Dubai; emergency treatment is free here. A consultation with a doctor in non-emergency cases costs around Dhs100. For emergencies with children, Latifa (formerly Al Wasl) Hospital (tel: 04 324 1111), across the highway from Wafi City, is a renowned paediatric hospital.

Dental problems can be dealt with by the American Dental Clinic (tel: 04 344 0668, www.americandentalclinic.com) or My Dental Clinic (tel: 04 338 8939, www.mydentalclinic.ae).

L

LANGUAGE

Arabic is the official language in the UAE, but English is widely spoken. It is unlikely that you will encounter any difficulty using English in hotels, restaurants or shops, as many of the staff are not Arabic-speakers themselves. That said, wherever you meet someone you know is an Arabic-speaker, it would be polite to have a few words and phrases committed to memory.

hello **marhaba**
welcome **ahlan wa-sahlan (ahlan)**
peace be with you (greeting) **as-salaam alaykum**
and with you be peace (response) **wa-alaykum as-salaam**
good morning **sabah al khayr**
good morning (response) **sabah al nour**
good evening **masaa al khayr**
good evening (response) **masaa al nour**
My name is... **ana ismi...**

What is your name? **shou ismac?**
How are you? **kayf haalak?**
well **zein**
please **min fadlak**
thank you **shukran**
yes/no **naam/la**
finished (as in I have ... or it is ...) **khallas**
goodbye, peace be with you **maa as-salaama**

LGBTQ TRAVELLERS

Homosexuality is not tolerated in the UAE and is officially illegal, so discretion is strongly advised.

M

MEDIA

The press in the UAE is not officially censored, although local journalists usually steer well clear of expressing negative or controversial opinions about local matters. Local English-language newspapers include the broadsheet *Gulf News* (www.gulfnews.com), *Khaleej Times* (www.khaleejtimes.com), *The Gulf Today* (www.gulftoday.ae), the tabloid *Emirates Today* (www.emirates247.com) and *7 Days* (www.7daysindubai.com). The best local newspaper is *The National* (www.thenational.ae), which is published in Abu Dhabi.

The main sources of information on events, concerts and hotel functions in the UAE are *What's On* (www.whatson.ae) and *Time Out Dubai* (www.timeoutdubai.com).

Note that imported magazines are often censored, with any material the authorities deem offensive struck through with a black marker.

The main English-language TV stations are Dubai's One (www.dcn.ae/dubaione) and Ajman TV (www.ajmantv.com). These show imported serials and English-language films; most also have English news.

International satellite TV stations including CNN and BBC World News are almost always available on hotel TVs.

Dubai has a number of English-language radio stations, including Virgin Radio Dubai (104.4FM; www.virginradiodubai.com) and Dubai 92 (92FM; www.dubai92.com).

MONEY

The currency in Dubai is the UAE dirham (Dhs or AED), which is pegged to the US dollar at the rate of Dhs3.6731 to US$1. There are 100 fils in a dirham. The notes in circulation are Dhs 5, 10, 20, 50, 100, 200, 500 and 1,000. Generally, it's good to carry Dhs100 notes and lower values for day-to-day transactions. The most common coins are the silver Dhs1, 50 fils and 25 fils.

Banks are generally open Sat–Thu 8am–1pm, closed Fri. The best places to change foreign currency and traveller's cheques into dirhams, however, are the numerous exchanges found in malls and souks, which keep shop hours. The main chains are Al Ansari Exchange (tel: 600 54 6000; www.alansariexchange.com), Al Fardan Exchange (tel: 600 522265; www.alfardanexchange.com), and Thomas Cook Al Rostamani (tel: 800 4250; www.alrostamaniexchange.com). Hotels may exchange cash and traveller's cheques at non-competitive rates for guests.

Major international credit and debit cards are accepted in large shops, restaurants and hotels. When shopping in souks, it's better to bargain for the 'best price' with cash.

O

OPENING HOURS

While Thursday afternoon and Friday are the weekend in the Islamic world, the local weekend in Dubai is Fri–Sat. Friday equates to a Sunday in the West. Banks and many private companies keep business hours on Saturdays.

Generally, government ministries and departments, most embassies and consulates are open Sun–Thu 7.30am–2.30pm, closed Fri–Sat. Many private-sector companies now follow the Western working hours of 9am–6pm, though some offices stick to the traditional split shift, with an extended lunch break between 1 and 4pm; these businesses start earlier, at 8am and close later, at 7pm. During Ramadan, fasting Muslims take a shorter working day and some businesses change their hours accordingly.

P

PHOTOGRAPHY

Visitors should ask permission before taking photos of Emiratis in national dress. Generally, Emirati women do not like having their picture taken, even when covered. The best place to photograph local men and women is the Heritage and Diving Village in Dubai or at Hatta Heritage Village, where they are used to the attention. Note that you should not take photos of government buildings or military bases, and that photography is not allowed at Dubai International Airport.

POLICE

Dubai's police force has a low-key but visible presence in the emirate – its green and white BMW and Mercedes patrol cars are a common sight. During rush hour, the traffic flow at busy intersections is often managed by police motorcyclists. The emergency number for the police is 999, while non-emergency inquiries can be made on 901. The toll-free number for general information, including details about the force's Department for Tourist Security, is 800 4438. The police website is www.dubaipolice.gov.ae.

POST OFFICES

Dubai's Central Post Office (Sat–Thu 7.30am–9pm) is located on Zabeel Road in Karama. There are smaller post offices scattered around the city, including Deira (near the Avari Hotel), Satwa (near Ravi's restaurant), Jumeirah (on Al Wasl Road) and at Dubai airport.

PUBLIC HOLIDAYS

There are eight public holidays in Dubai. Two fall on fixed dates, the others move date year-on-year according to the Islamic calendar, shifting by (usually) 11 days each year.

New Year's Day **Jan 1**

UAE National Day **Dec 2**

Moveable holidays

Moloud (Prophet Mohammed's Birthday)

Lailat Al Mi'Raj (Ascent of the Prophet)

Eid Al Fitr (end of Ramadan)

Arafat Day (beginning of the pilgrimage to Mecca)

Eid Al Adha (Feast of the Sacrifice)

Al Hijra (Islamic New Year)

PUBLIC TRANSPORT

Almost all public transport in Dubai – metro, buses and waterbuses (but not *abras*) is covered by the Nol integrated ticket system (www.nol.ae). You will need to get a pre-paid Nol card before you can use any of these. Cards can be bought (or topped up) at any metro station, at numerous bus stops, or at branches of Carrefour, Spinneys, Waitrose and the Emirates NBD Bank. There are four different types of card/ticket. The Red Ticket has been specially designed for visitors, costing just Dhs2, and can be topped up with 10 single fares for one mode of transport (bus or metro); you might prefer to invest in a more flexible Silver Card (Dhs25, including Dhs19 credit), which stores up to Dhs5000 of credit and lasts five years.

Metro Dubai's new state-of-the-art Metro system (www.rta.ae) has revolutionized travel within the city since opening in 2009, making getting around far easier – and cheaper – than before. The system comprises a mix of overground and underground lines, with bright modern stations, although the popularity of the system means that it is often surprisingly difficult to get a seat.

There are two lines currently open. The Red Line runs from Rashidiya via the airport and old city and then down through Karama and along

Sheikh Zayed Road all the way to Jebel Ali, at the far southern edge of the city. The Green Line loops around the old city centre through Deira and Bur Dubai. By 2020, there will be an extension to the Red Line running to the Expo site. The metro system is gradually being developed; there are various plans for new extensions and lines. Trains run approximately every 10 minutes, Sat–Wed 5am–midnight (Green Line runs from 5.30am), Thu until 1am, Fri 10am–1am. Fares start at Dhs3 up to Dhs7.5 in standard class, or from Dhs8 to Dhs17 in the superior Gold Class, which offers slightly plusher carriages.

Tram Launched in November 2014, the Dubai Tram operates between Al Sufouh and Jumeirah Lakes Towers, with stops including the Dubai Marina and Palm Jumeirah. It takes 36 minutes to ride the entire line. A single fare is Dhs3, and Nol cards can be used. For more information see www.rta.ae.

Bus Dubai's bus service is not generally very useful for trips within the city for visitors (for routes see http://dubai-buses.com). For trips to other emirates, there are regular and reliable services from Al Ghubaibah Bus Station in Bur Dubai to Abu Dhabi, Al Ain, Sharjah and (less frequently) Hatta.

Taxi This remains the best way of getting around the areas of the city that the metro has not yet reached. Cabs are metered, air-conditioned, mostly reliable and can be flagged down on the street, or pre-booked. Taxis from the airport start with the meter at Dhs20, though in the city, meters start at Dhs10. The main operators are Dubai Taxi (tel: 04 208 0000; www.dubaitaxi.ae), Cars Taxis (tel: 800 8294; www.carstaxi.ae) and National Taxis (tel: 04 327 4666; www.nationaltaxi.ae). Note that street names are rarely used in Dubai except for the biggest roads, navigation is usually by local landmarks; this is how taxi drivers will expect to be directed, rather than being given a street address.

Waterbus or *Abra* Dubai is split in two by the Creek, which can be crossed (most memorably) by *abra* or, alternatively, waterbus. Air-conditioned waterbuses serve various points on the Creek, costing Dhs3–5 per return journey, payable only with a Nol card. They are much less enjoyable than the city's *abras*, however, and at double the price have little to recommend them.

R

RELIGION

Islam is the official religion of the UAE, but there is freedom of worship for Christians in church compounds, on the understanding that they do not proselytise. The main church services are held on Friday – the local weekend. Bibles for personal use can be carried into the country.

All Muslims, except young children, the elderly and pregnant women, observe Ramadan, which lasts 29 or 30 days each year. During this month they abstain from food and drink (and smoking and sex) from sunrise to sunset. Most hotel restaurants will serve food to visitors during the daytime (often screening tables from public view) but you should be sensitive not to eat or drink (or chew gum) in public during this holy month. The dates for Ramadan move each year, following the Islamic calendar.

T

TELEPHONE

The international dialling code for the UAE is 00 971. The code for Dubai landlines is 04 – overseas callers should drop the 0. Calls within Dubai are free. The code for UAE mobile phones is 050, 055 or 056 – again, overseas callers should drop the first 0.

Etisalat payphones (card- or coin-operated) can be found in malls, usually near the prayer room or toilet area. Pre-paid phone cards are available from Etisalat, supermarkets and service stations.

As charges for international mobile roaming are high, consider buying a local prepaid card for longer stays. Emirati mobile network operators include Etisalat (www.etisalat.ae) and Du (www.du.ae).

TIME ZONE

Dubai is four hours ahead of GMT/Universal Coordinated Time (UCT), throughout the year.

New York	London	Jo'burg	**Dubai**	Sydney	Auckland
3am	8am	10am	**noon**	7pm	9pm

TIPPING
Tipping is appreciated, but not expected. A 10 percent service charge is often added automatically to bills, although this is not necessarily shared with staff – better to leave cash if you wish to express your appreciation. Tipping in taxis is not expected, although many visitors often round up the fare and let the driver keep the change.

TOILETS
Western-style toilets are commonly found in hotels and restaurants. In malls and other public gathering places there is usually a combination of Western-style and squat toilets.

TOURIST INFORMATION (see also Guides and tours)
The Government of Dubai Department of Tourism and Commerce Marketing (DTCM; tel: 04 282 1111; www.visitdubai.com) is the emirate's official tourism promotion organisation. DTCM's information centres in Dubai include kiosks in Terminals 1 and 2 at Dubai International Airport, and desks in the following malls: Deira City Centre, BurJuman Centre, Wafi City, Mercato and Ibn Battuta. The head office is on floors 6–9 of Al Fattan Plaza on Airport Road.

UK 4th Floor, Nuffield House, 41–46 Piccadilly, London W10DS; tel: 020 7321 6110; e-mail: dtcm_uk@ dubaitourism.ae.

North America tel: +9711 600 55 5559; e-mail: jessica.herring@dubai tourism.ae .

Australia & New Zealand Level 14, Suites 5 & 6, 3 Spring Street, Sydney, NSW 2000; tel: +61 2 9956 6620; e-mail: dtcm_aus@dubai tourism.ae.

South Africa tel: +971 600 55 5559; e-mail: dtcm_sa@ dubaitourism.ae.

TRAVELLERS WITH DISABILITIES

Dubai is one of the Middle East's most accessible destinations. Most of the city's more upmarket hotels now have specially adapted rooms for disabled travellers, and some of the city's malls include disabled parking spaces and specially equipped toilets. Transport is also fairly well adapted. Dubai Taxi (tel: 04 208 0000; www.dubaitaxi.ae) has specially designed vehicles equipped with ramps and lifts, while the Metro features tactile guide paths, lifts and ramps to assist visually- and mobility-impaired visitors, as well as wheelchair spaces in all compartments. The city's waterbuses can also be used by mobility-impaired visitors, and staff will assist you in boarding and disembarking, while there are also dedicated facilities for passengers with special needs at the airport. Sadly, but not surprisingly, most of the city's older heritage buildings are not accessible (although the Dubai Museum is an exception).

W

WEBSITES AND INTERNET ACCESS

The following websites are useful sources of information:
www.arabianbusiness.com Arabian Business
www.emirates247.com Emirates 24/7 news portal
www.dm.gov.ae Dubai Municipality
www.dubaiairports.ae Dubai International Airports
www.visitdubai.com Government of Dubai Department of Tourism and Commerce Marketing
www.sheikhmohammed.co.ae Sheikh Mohammed Bin Rashid Al Maktoum
    Internet connections are available in the guest rooms and business centres of larger hotels; also in many restaurants, cafés, shopping malls, parks and beaches and on the Dubai Metro. Note that access to certain websites may be blocked in Dubai due to political, religious or sexual content.

WEIGHTS AND MEASURES

Dubai (and the UAE) uses the metric system.

RECOMMENDED HOTELS

Accommodation in Dubai doesn't come cheap, but standards at the city's top hotels rival anywhere in the world, offering unparalleled levels of style and luxury. Broadly speaking, hotels divide into beach-front resort-style hotels, almost all of which are located in the southern part of the city, and business-oriented hotels, the best of which can be found strung along or near to Sheikh Zayed Road. There are also a handful of good places in or around the old city centre. There is plenty of cheaper accommodation in the areas around the Creek as well, although standards are more basic.

The accommodation listed below ranges from inexpensive holiday apartments to icons of contemporary opulence like the Burj Al Arab (popularly dubbed the world's first 'seven-star' hotel). The price categories indicated by $ symbols next to the hotel name include an additional 20 percent tax and service charge where this is applicable, but if you telephone a hotel yourself, in most cases the figure you will be quoted will not include this 20 percent. In many hotels, the rate includes a complimentary buffet breakfast, otherwise it is an additional Dhs75–100.

The price categories below are based on the high-season rate for a standard room for two people. They do not indicate star rating.

$$$$	Dhs3,500–8,000
$$$	Dhs2,500–3,500
$$	Dhs1,000–2,500
$	Under Dhs1,000

DUBAI

The coast

Al Qasr $$$$ *Madinat Jumeirah, tel: 04 366 8888,* www.jumeirah.com. Its Arabic name means 'The Palace', and this grand boutique hotel really is fit for a king. Part of the Arabian-style Madinat Jumeirah resort next to Burj Al Arab, Al Qasr boasts a palatial gated entrance and opulent interiors, and shares 1km (0.5 mile) of beach with the resort's other hotel, Mina A'Salam. Its restaurants include the excellent Pierchic, located at the end of a wooden pier jutting into the Gulf from the hotel's gardens. For extra privacy, 29 summer houses, located around a picturesque network of canals, are also available.

Atlantis The Palm $$$ *Palm Jumeirah, tel: 04 426 0000,* www.atlantisthepalm.com. Having opened in style with a launch party that saw Hollywood's A-listers walk down the red carpet, this popular themed resort houses 1,373 lavish guest rooms and 166 suites – including the Lost Chambers, with their mesmerising underwater views. With a dazzling mix of leisure facilities, retail outlets and eateries like Nobu and Ossiano, Atlantis has become an iconic tourist attraction.

Burj Al Arab $$$$ *Umm Suqeim, tel: 04 301 7777,* www.jumeirah. com. A stay in this iconic 'seven-star' hotel offers the last word in opulence, with every mod-con and indulgence you could imagine (and several you probably couldn't), ranging from remote-control curtains to 'pillow menus'. Suites are huge, butlers come as standard and the whole place screams luxury, although at an inevitably stratospheric price – you'll be stretched to find a room for much less than $2,000 a night.

Dubai Marine Beach Resort & Spa $$ *Jumeira Road, Jumeira 1, tel: 04 346 1111,* www.dxbmarine.com. Not to be confused with Dubai Marina along the coast, Dubai Marine is the closest beach resort to the city, a short walk across Jumeirah Road from Jumeirah Mosque. It offers 195 rooms in villa-style low-rise buildings in a landscaped compound fronting on to a small beach. It also has some of the city's best nightspots, including Sho Cho and Boudoir.

Grosvenor House $$ *Dubai Marina, tel: 04 399 8888,* www.grosvenorhouse-dubai.com. Although it is not located on the beach, this 45-storey Starwood Hotels and Resorts property offers stunning views of the coast, including The Palm Jumeirah and Dubai Marina. Guests can use the beach facilities at the nearby Le Royal Meridien Beach Resort. Notable nightspots at the hotel include Buddha Bar and Bar 44.

Jumeirah Beach Hotel $$$ *Umm Suqeim, tel: 04 348 0000,* www.jumei rah.com. Shaped like a breaking wave to complement nearby Burj Al Ar- ab's 'sail', the 26-storey landmark is one of the best beachside hotels in Dubai for both families and couples, with stunning architecture, excellent family facilities, superb grounds and a plethora of restaurants and bars.

Jumeirah Zabeel Saray $$$ *The Palm Jumeirah, tel: 04 453 0000,* www. jumeirah.com. One of the first hotels to open on the outer breakwater of The Palm Jumeirah, this opulent new place has lavish Ottoman styling, with a range of beautifully designed rooms and villas, plus the sumptuous Talise Ottoman Spa and a clutch of excellent eating and drinking venues.

Le Royal Meridien $$$ *Dubai Marina, tel: 04 399 5555,* www.leroyalme ridien-dubai.com. This old resort hotel lacks the style of nearby estab- lishments but compensates with superb outdoor facilities – a huge pool, vast gardens and a superb swathe of beach. One of the best hotels in the city for families.

Mina A'Salam $$$$ *Madinat Jumeirah, tel: 04 366 8888,* www.jumei rah.com. A shade less expensive than the nearby Al Qasr, the Madinat Jumeirah resort's second grand hotel impresses with its fabulous faux- Arabian architecture and waterfront setting. Mina A'Salam is connected via canals and walkways to Souk Madinat Jumeirah, making its cafés, restaurants and bars more accessible.

One&Only Royal Mirage $$$ *Al Sufouh Road, Al Sufouh, tel: 04 399 9999,* www.oneandonlyresorts.com. Until Madinat Jumeirah opened in 2004, the Royal Mirage was the only hotel on the coast that could offer an Ara- bian (or, at least, Moroccan) look and feel, and despite the competition it still takes some beating. Located on 1km (0.5 mile) of waterfront, the Royal Mirage offers 250 rooms in the Palace, 170 in the Arabian Court and 50 in the exclusive Residence & Spa. The hotel's venues include the excellent Eauzone and Tagine restaurant, Rooftop bar and Kasbar nightclub, plus a superb spa.

The Ritz-Carlton Dubai $$$ *Dubai Marina, tel: 04 399 4000,* www.ritzcarlton. com. A little bit of Andalusia in the Gulf, the low-lying hacienda-style Ritz-

Carlton has 138 rooms, all sea-facing. More than any other hotel on the coast, it is a quiet retreat for rest and relaxation, far removed from the distractions and crowds of larger beach resorts. In-house amenities include the highly rated French-style La Baie fine-dining restaurant.

Sheikh Zayed Road

Armani Hotel $$$ *Burj Khalifa, Downtown Dubai, tel: 04 888 3888* www. armanihoteldubai.com. Occupying the lower floors of the Burj Khalifa, the world's first Armani hotel offers pretty much the last word in designer minimalism and luxury.

Fairmont Dubai $$ *Sheikh Zayed Road, tel: 04 332 5555,* www.fairmont. com. Located at the northern end of Sheikh Zayed Road, the Fairmont is one of the most luxurious hotels along the road, with plush rooms, a fancy spa and a pair of fourth-floor pools. The space-age interior boasts the award-winning Exchange Grills restaurant. There are also seven other dining venues.

Ibis World Trade Centre $ *Sheikh Zayed Road/Trade Centre 2, tel: 04 332 4444,* www.accorhotels.com. This simple but comfortable four-star is perhaps the best-value hotel in the city, although rooms can get booked up quickly if there is a big event on at the Dubai World Trade Centre which is located next door.

Jumeirah Emirates Towers Hotel $$$ *Sheikh Zayed Road, tel: 04 330 0000,* www.jumeirah.com. Part of the Jumeirah Group's portfolio, the landmark 305m (1,000ft) Emirates Towers Hotel has frequently been voted one of the world's best business hotels. Each of the 400 rooms, over 51 floors, has a dedicated workstation with ultra high-speed internet connection, wireless keyboard and fax/printer with private number. Its numerous bars and restaurants include the Italian Alta Badia, the separate Alta Badia Bar and The Agency.

The Palace Downtown Dubai $$$ *Emaar Boulevard, The Old Town Island, Downtown Dubai, tel: 04 428 7888,* www.addresshotels.com. The Palace is exactly what the name suggests – an opulent hotel reminiscent of an old Arabian palace. Only in this case, the traditional Arabesque facade is complemented with contemporary interiors that are no less luxurious than you would expect in a royal palace. It has views of the Dubai Fountain and the marvellous Burj Khalifa, and is close to Dubai Mall, as well as the business districts. There are three restaurants, including the excellent Thiptara.

Shangri-La Hotel $$ *Sheikh Zayed Road, tel: 04 343 8888*, www.shangri-la.com. The most appealing hotel on Sheikh Zayed Road, set in a towering, Gotham-esque structure at the southern end of the strip. Inside the hotel is a model of Zen cool, with beautiful rooms (many with outstanding views) and a string of excellent restaurants.

Bur Dubai

Arabian Courtyard $ *Al Fahidi St, Bur Dubai, tel: 04 351 9111*, www.arabiancourtyard.com. Overlooking the Dubai Museum, this attractive four-star could hardly be more central or better positioned for forays into the old city centre. Inside, there are attractive rooms with Arabian touches and some good eating and drinking spots.

Four Points by Sheraton Bur Dubai $ *Khalid Bin Al Waleed Street (Bank Street), tel: 04 397 7444*, www.fourpointsburdubai.com. Right in the heart of the old city, this comfortable and competitively priced four-star makes an excellent base for exploring Bur Dubai and Deira. It also boasts good facilities, including the lovely Antique Bazaar restaurant and the cosy Viceroy Pub.

Golden Sands $ *Between Mankhool Road and Sheikh Khalifa Bin Zayed Road (Trade Centre Road), tel: 04 355 0000*, www.goldensandsdubai.com. A vast number of pleasant self-catering studios and apartments scattered over 11 separate buildings in the Al Mankhool area of Bur Dubai – often some of the cheapest lodgings in town, if you don't mind foregoing traditional hotel facilities.

Grand Hyatt Dubai $$ *Sheikh Rashid Road, Umm Hurair, tel: 04 317 2206*, www.dubai.grand.hyatt.com. A rare resort-type hotel in the centre of the

city, the 674-room Grand Hyatt lies roughly halfway between the airport and Sheikh Zayed Road. The central location makes the hotel a good base for sightseeing or business meetings on either side of the Creek. The hotel is also convenient for Wafi and for zipping along Route 44 towards Al Ain or the Hatta road.

XVA Hotel $ *Al Fahidi Historical Neighbourhood, tel: 04 353 5383,* www. xvahotel.com. No other paid accommodation in Dubai can compete with the XVA Gallery's authentic Arabian offering. More a guesthouse than a hotel – too small to qualify for a star rating – the XVA is first and foremost an art gallery and coffee shop set around the inner courtyard of a restored home in the Al Fahidi Historical Neighbourhood. It has 13 guest rooms, furnished in Arabian style, some on the first-floor rooftop, which offers wonderful views of the Creek skyline and the wind-towers on nearby buildings.

Deira

Hilton Dubai Creek $$ *Baniyas Road, tel: 04 227 1111,* www3.hilton.com. Designed by Carlos Ott, the 154-room Hilton Dubai Creek is a stylish, contemporary hotel set back on the land side of Baniyas Road. It has outstanding views of the nearby dhow wharves as well as of the distant Sheikh Zayed Road skyline from its Creek-facing rooms.

Hyatt Regency Dubai $$ *Corniche Road, tel: 04 209 1234,* www.dubai. regency.hyatt.com. A distinctive dark monolith overlooking the mouth of Dubai Creek, this is one of the city's oldest five-stars, although refurbishments have kept things fresh. All rooms have sea views, while popular in-house restaurants include the Iranian Shahrzad and the Japanese Miyako. The hotel also has Dubai's only revolving restaurant, the rooftop Al Dawaar.

Park Hyatt $$$ *Dubai Creek Golf & Yacht Club, tel: 04 602 1234,* www.dubai. park.hyatt.com. Rivalling the nearby Raffles for the title of the city centre's top place to stay, this idyllic city retreat occupies a sprawl of Moroccan-style buildings spread along the Creek between the Dubai Creek and Golf clubs. The hotel has gorgeous Arabian styling and superb views.

Radisson Blu $ *Baniyas Road, tel: 04 222 7171,* www.radissonblu.com/hotel-dubaideiracreek. This was the first chain hotel in Dubai when it opened as the InterContinental in 1975. The 276-room Radisson Blu remains a firm favourite thanks to its central location overlooking the creek. Among the hotel's venues are the hip Asian eatery YUM! and Up On The 10th, one of the best live jazz venues in town. The dhow wharves are within walking distance and the Deira souks are a short cab ride away.

Raffles $$$ *Sheikh Rashid Rd, Wafi, tel: 04 324 8888,* www.raffles.com. A spectacular hotel housed in a giant pyramid with a mix of quirky Egyptian theming and cool Asian designs. This hotel offers superb facilities including huge gardens, a gorgeous spa and some excellent restaurants and bars.

Outside the city

Al Maha Desert Resort & Spa $$$$ *Interchange No. 8, Dubai–Al Ain Road, tel: 04 832 9900,* www.al-maha.com. The Al Maha eco-resort, 40km (25 miles) from Dubai, is a world-class destination with prices to match. Resembling a luxury tented camp within the 225 sq km (87 sq mile) Dubai Desert Conservation Reserve, the 'six-star' resort is named after the Arabian oryx *(al maha)* that live and breed in the surrounding dunes. Each of its 40 suites has a private pool. Horse riding, camel trekking and falconry are among the activities on offer for guests; there is also an alluring spa.

Bab al Shams Desert Resort & Spa $$ *Endurance City, tel: 04 809 6100,* www.babalshams.com. If the budget won't stretch to Al Maha, consider Bab al Shams (literally 'Gate of the Sun'). The opulent fort-style building is set among the dunes not far from Dubai's centre for endurance riding and 37km (23 miles) from Dubai Autodrome.

Hatta Fort Hotel $$ *Hatta, tel: 04 809 9333,* www.jaresortshotels.com. Before the Al Maha resort and Bab al Shams, the four-star Hatta Fort Hotel was the only retreat from the city that promised some luxury. Set among the mountains of the Hajar range, an hour's drive from Dubai near the border with Oman, the Hatta Fort may be a little dated now, but its appeal is enduring. Its 50 chalets have views of the mountains which can be explored on 4x4 trips arranged by the hotel.

DICTIONARY

ENGLISH – ARABIC

adj adjective   **adv** adverb   **BE** British English   **n** noun   **prep** preposition   **v** verb

A

accept يقبل yaqbal
access مدخل madkhal
access v **(internet)** يدخل yadkhul
accident حادث Haadith
accompany يرافق yuraafiq
account حساب Hisaab
acetaminophen سيتامول seetaamool
acupuncture علاج بالإبر ʻilaaj bil-ibar
adapter محوّل muHawwil
address عنوان ʻunwaan
admission رسم الدخول (to museum etc) rasm ad-dukhool
after بعد baʻad
afternoon بعد الظهر baʻad aZ-Zuhr
aftershave عطر بعد الحلاقة ʻuTr baʻad al-Halaaqa
age عمر ʻumr
agency وكالة wakaala
AIDS أيدز aydz
air conditioner مكيف الهواء mukayyif al-hawaaʼ
airline خطوط جوية khuToot jaweeya
airplane طائرة Taaʼira
airport مطار maTaar
air pump منفاخ minfaakh
aisle seat مقعد على الممشى maqʻad ʻala al-mamsha
Algeria الجزائر al-jazaaʼir
Algerian جزائري jazaaʼiree
allergic يعاني من الحساسية yuʻaanee min al-Hasaaseeya
allowed مسموح masmooH
alone بمفرده bi-munfaridih
alter يعدل yuʻaddil
alternate route طريق آخر Tareeq aakhar
aluminum foil رقائق الألمنيوم raqaaʼiq aluminyoom
amazing مدهش mud-hish
ambulance سيارة الإسعاف sayaarat al-isʻaaf
American adj أمريكي amreekee

amusement park مدينة الملاهي madeenat al-malaahee
anemic مصاب بفقر الدم muSaab bi-fuqr ad-damm
anesthesia تخدير takhdeer
animal حيوان Haywaan
ankle كاحل kaaHil
another آخر aakhar
antibiotics المضادات الحيوية muDadaat al-Hayawaya
antiques store محل الأنتيكات maHal al-anteekaat
antiseptic cream كريم معقم kreem muʻaqim
anything أي شيء ay shay
apartment شقة shiqqa
appendix الزائدة الدودية az-zaaʼidat ad-doodeeya
appointment موعد mawʻid
Arab (person) عربي ʻarabee
Arabic adj عربي ʻarabee; n **(language)** العربية al-ʻarabeeya
arcade قاعة الألعاب qaaʻat al-alʻaab
area code رمز المنطقة ramz al-manTaqa
arm ذراع dhiraaʻ
aromatherapy علاج أروماتي ʻilaaj aroomaatee
arrivals (airport) الوصول al-wuSool
arrive يصل yaSil
arthritis التهاب مفاصل iltihaab mafaaSil
aspirin أسبرين asbireen
assistance مساعدة musaaʻada
asthmatic مريض الربو mareeD bir-rabu
ATM الصراف الآلي aS-Saraaf al-aalee
attack (on person) اعتداء iʻtidaaʼ
attraction (sightseeing) المعلم الرئيسية al-maʻallim ar-raʼeeseeya
attractive (person) جذاب jadhaab
Australia أستراليا ustraaleeyaa
Australian أسترالي ustralaee
automatic أوتوماتيكي awtoomaateekee
available غير مشغول ghayr mashghool

B

baby رضيع raDee'
baby bottle رضّاعة riDaa'a
baby food طعام للرضع Ta'aam lir-raDa'
babysitter مربية أطفال murabeeyat aTfaal
baby wipe محارم للطفل maHaarim liT-Tifl
back (of body) ظهر Zuhr
backache ألم في الظهر alam fee iZ-Zuhr
backpack حقيبة ظهر Haqeeba Zuhr
bad رديء radee'
bag كيس kees
baggage claim استلام الحقائب istilaam al-Haqaa'ib
Bahrain البحرين al-baHrayn
Bahraini بحريني baHraynee
bakery المخبز al-makhbaz
ballet عرض باليه 'arD baalayh
bandage ضمادات Damaadaat
ban بنك bank
bar بار baar
barber حلاق رجالي Halaaq rijaalee
baseball البايسبول al-baysbool
basket سلة silla
basketball كرة السلة kurrat as-silla
bathroom حمام Hamaam
battery بطارية baTaareeya
be يكون yakoon
beach شاطئ shaaTee'
beautiful جميل jameel
bed سرير sareer
before قبل qabl
begin يبدأ yabda'
beginner مبتدئ mubtadi'
behind خلف khalf
beige بيج bayj
belt حزام Hizaam
best الأحسن al-aHsan
bet n مراهنة muraahana
better أفضل afDal
bicycle دراجة daraaja
big كبير kabeer
bikini wax شمع خط البيكيني shama' khaT al-beekeenee
bill n حساب Hisaab
bird طير Tayr
birthday عيد ميلاد 'eed meelaad
black أسود aswad

bladder مثانة mathaana
blanket بطانية baTaaneeya
bleed ينزف yanzif
blender خلاط khalaaT
blood دم damm
blood pressure ضغط الدم DaghuT ad-damm
blouse بلوزة blooza
blue أزرق azraq
boarding pass بطاقة صعود biTaaqat Su'ood
boat قارب qaarib
boat trip رحلة بالقارب riHla bil-qaarib
bone عظم 'aZm
book كتاب kitaab
bookstore مكتبة maktaba
boot جزمة jazma
boring ممل mumill
botanical garden حديقة النباتات Hadeeqat an-nabaataat
bottle زجاجة zujaaja
bottle opener فتاحة زجاجات fataaHa zujaajaat
bowl زبدية zubdeeya
box علبة 'ulba
boxing ملاكمة mulaakama
boy صبي Sabee
boyfriend صاحب SaaHib
bra حمالة صدر Hamaala Sadr
bracelet سوار siwaar
brake فرامل faraamil
break (tooth, bone) يكسر yukassir
breakdown تعطل ta'Tul
breakfast فطور fuToor
break-in اقتحام iqtiHaam
breast ثدي thaddee
breastfeed ترضع turaDDi'
breath يتنفس yatanaffas
bridge جسر jisr
briefs سروال داخلي sirwaal daakhilee
bring يجلب yajlib
British adj بريطاني breeTaanee
broken مكسور maksoor
brooch بروش broosh
broom مكنسة miknasa
brother أخ akh
brown بني bunnee
bugs حشرات Hasharaat
building مبنى mabna

burn n حرق Harq
bus باص baaS
bus station محطة الباص maHaTat al-baaS
bus stop موقف الباص mawqif al-baaS
bus ticket تذكرة للباص tadhkara lil-baaS
bus tour جولة بالباص jawla bil-baaS
business أعمال a'maal
business card كرت الأعمال kart al-a'maal
business center مركز الأعمال markaz al-a'maal
business class درجة الأعمال darajat al-a'maal
business hours أوقات العمل awqaat al-'amal
busy مشغول mashghool
butcher لحام laHaam
butter زبدة zibda
buttock ردفين ridfayn
buy v يشتري yashtaree
bye مع السلامة ma' as-salaama

c

cabin كابينة kaabeena
cafe مقهى maqha
call (telephone) يتصل yattaSil
call collect كلفة المكالمة على المتصل kulfat al-mukaalama 'ala al-muttaSil
calorie حريرات Hurayraat
camera كاميرا kaameeraa
camera store محل الكاميرات maHal al-kaameeraat
camp v يخيم yukhayyam
camping stove فرن مخيم furn mukhayyam
campsite مخيم mukhayyam
Canada كندا kanadaa
Canadian كندي kanadee
cancel الغي alghee
car سيارة sayaara
car hire [BE] تأجير السيارات ta'jeer as-sayaaraat
car park [BE] موقف السيارات mawqif as-sayaaraat
car rental تأجير السيارات ta'jeer as-sayaaraat
car seat مقعد سيارة maq'ad sayaara
carafe إبريق ibreeq
card بطاقة biTaaqa
carry-on (piece of hand luggage) حقيبة يد Haqeeba yad
cart (for luggage, shopping) عربة 'araba
carton كرتونة kartoona
cash كاش kaash
cash advance دفعة مسبقة duf'a musabbaqa

cashier محاسب muHaasib
casino كازينو kazeenoo
castle قلعة qal'a
cave كهف kahf
CD سي دي see dee
cell phone هاتف نقال haatif naqaal
Celsius سلسيوس silseeyoos
centimeter سنتمتر centimeter
certificate شهادة shahaada
chair كرسي kursee
change v (baby) يغير حفاض الطفل yughayir HifaaD aT-Tifl; v (money) يبدل yubaddil; v (travel) يغير yughayir
charcoal فحم faHm
charge v (cost) سعر si'r; v يطلب yaTlub
cheap رخيص rakheeS
check (in restaurant) حساب Hisaab; n (payment) شيك sheek; v يفحص yafHaS; n (luggage) يودع الأمتعة yuwadi' al-amti'a
check-in إجراءات السفر ijra'aat as-safar
checking account حساب الجاري Hisaab al-jaaree
check-out (from hotel) مغادرة الفندق mughaadarat al-funduq
chemical toilet تواليت كيميائي at-toowaaleet al-kimiyaa'ee
chemist [BE] صيدلية Saydleeya
cheque [BE] شيك sheek
chest صدر Sadr
chest pain ألم في الصدر alam fee iS-Sadr
chewing gum علكة 'ilka
child طفل Tifl
children's menu قائمة طعام للأطفال qaa'imat Ta'aam lil-aTfaal
children's portion وجبات أصغر للأطفال wajabaat aSghar lil-aTfaal
child's seat كرسي خاص للأطفال kursee khaaS lil-aTfaal
chopsticks عيدان صينية للأكل 'eedaan Seeneeya lil-akul
church كنيسة kaneesa
cigar سيجار seegaar
cigarette سجائر sijaa'ir
claim form استمارة مطالبة istimaara muTaalaba
class (in school) صف Saff
classical music موسيقى كلاسيكية mooseeqa klaaseekeeya
clean adj نظيف naZeef
cleaning supplies مواد تنظيف mawaad tanZeef

cliff منحدر munHadar

cling film [BE] غلاف نايلون ghilaaf naayloon

clock ساعة حائطية saa'a Haa'iTeeya

close (near) قرب qareeb; v يغلق yaghliq

closed مغلق mughlaq

clothes ملابس malaabis

clothing store محل الملابس maHal al-malaabis

club نادي naadee

coat معطف mi'Taf

coffee shop مقهى maqha

coin قطعة نقدية qiT'a naqdeeya

colander مصفاة miSfaah

cold adj بارد baariq; n (illness) رشح rashH

colleague زميل zameel

cologne كولونيا kooloonyaa

color صبغة Sabgha

comb مشط mishT

come يأتي ya'tee

complaint شكوى shakwa

computer كومبيوتر kumbyootir

concert حفلة موسيقية Hafla mooseeqeeya

concert hall قاعة الحفلات الموسيقية qaa'at al-Haflaat al-mooseeqeeya

conditioner بلسم balsam

condom واقي ذكري waaqee dhikree

conference مؤتمر mu'tamar

confirm يؤكد yu'akid

congestion احتقان iHtiqaan

connect يتصل yuttaSil

connection (travel) تبديل طائرة tabdeel Taa'ira; (internet) اتصال ittiSaal

constipated مصاب بإمساك muSaab bi-imsaak

consulate قنصلية qunSuleeya

consultant مستشار mustashaar

contact v يتصل yuttaSil

contact lens عدسة لاصقة 'adasa laaSiqa

contact lens solution محلول للعدسات اللاصقة maHlool lil-'adasaat al-laaSiqa

contagious معد mu'din

convention hall قاعة المؤتمرات qaa'at al-mu'tamaraat

cook v يطبخ yaTbukh

cooking facilities لوازم طبخ lawaazim Tabkh

cooking gas غاز الطبخ ghaaz aT-Tabkh

cool (temperature) بارد قليلا baarid qaleelan

copper نحاس nuHaas

corkscrew فتاحة النبيذ fataaHat an-nabeedh

corner زاوية zaaweeya

cost v يكلف yukalif

cot سرير قابل للطوي sareer qaabil liT-Tawwi; [BE] سرير أطفال sareer aTfaal

cotton قطن quTn

cough n سعال su'aal

country code رمز البلد ramz al-balad

cover charge رسم الخدمة rasm al-khidma

cramps تشنج tashannuj

crash n (in car) حادث اصطدام Haadith iSTidaam

cream (ointment) مرهم marham

credit ائتمان i'timaan

credit card بطاقة ائتمان biTaaqat al-i'timaan

crew neck ياقة مدورة yaaqa mudawwara

crib سرير أطفال sareer aTfaal

crystal كريستال kreestaal

cup فنجان finjaan

currency عملة 'umla

currency exchange تبديل العملات tabdeel al-'umlaat

currency exchange office مكتب تبديل العملات maktab tabdeel al-'umlaat

customs الجمرك al-jumruk

customs declaration form تصريح جمركي taSreeH jumrukee

cut n جرح jurH; v (hair) يقص yaquSS

cute جميل jameel

cycling ركوب الدراجة rukoob ad-daraaja

D

dairy منتجات الألبان muntajaat al-albaan

damaged تالف taalif

dance v يرقص yarquS

dance club نادي للرقص naadee lir-raqS

dancing الرقص ar-raqS

dangerous خطير KhaTeer

dark غامق ghaamik

date (on calendar) تاريخ ta'reekh

day يوم yawm

deaf أصم aSam

debit سحب من الحساب الجاري saHab min al-Hisaab al-jaaree

deck chair كرسي للشاطئ kursee lish-shaaTee'

degrees (temperature) درجات darajaat

delay n يتأخر yata'akhar

delete v يمحي yamHi

delicatessen محل الأطعمة الفاخرة maHal al-
aT'imat al-faakhira
delicious لذيذ ladheedh
denim جينز jeenz
dentist طبيب أسنان Tabeeb asnaan
deodorant مزيل الرائحة muzeel ar-raa'iHa
department store محل تجاري maHal tijaaree
departure gate بوابات السفر bawaabaat as-safar
departures مغادرة mughaadara
deposit عربون 'arboon; **(at bank)** إيداع eedaa'
desert صحراء SaHraa'
detergent منظف munaZZif
detour تحويلة taHweela
develop (film) تحميض taHmeeD
diabetic مريض بالسكري mareeD bis-sukaree
dial v يضغط yiDghuT
diamond ألماس al-maas
diaper حفاظ HifaaZ
diarrhea إسهال is-haal
diesel ديزل deezil
difficult صعب Su'ub
digital ديجيتال dijeetaal
digital camera كاميرا ديجيتال kaameera dijeetaal
digital photo صور ديجيتال Suwwar dijeetaal
digital print صور ديجيتال Suwwar dijeetaal
dining room غرفة الطعام ghurfat aT-Ta'aam
dinner عشاء 'ashaa'
direction اتجاه itijaah
dirty وسخ wisikh
disabled معاق mu'aaq
disabled-accessible [BE] مكان مجهز لاستقبال
المعاقين makaan mujahhaz li-istiqbaal al-mu'aaqeen
disabled toilet [BE] توواليت خاص للمعاقين toowaaleet khaaS lil-mu'aaqeen
disconnect يقطع الاتصال yaqTa' al-ittiSaal
discount تخفيض takhfeeD
dish صحن SaHn
dishwasher غسالة الصحون ghasaalat aS-SuHoon
dishwashing liquid سائل لغسيل الصحون saa'il
li-ghaseel aS-SuHoon
display case فترينة fitreenaa
disposable موس الحلاقة للاستعمال مرة واحدة
moos al-Halaaqa lil-isti'maal marra waaHida
dive v يغطس yaghTus
diving equipment معدات الغوص mu'iddaat lil-ghawS
divorced مطلق muTallaq

dizzy يشعر بدوار yash'ur bi-duwaar
doctor طبيب Tabeeb
doll دمية dumya
dollar دولار doolaar
domestic محلي maHalee
door باب baab
dormitory غرفة نوم ghurfa nawm
double bed سرير مزدوج sareer muzdawwaj
double room غرفة مزدوجة ghurfa muzdawwaja
downtown (direction) باتجاه مركز المدينة bi-ittijah
markaz al-madeena
downtown area مركز المدينة markaz al-madeena
dozen دزينة duzeena
dress (woman's) فستان fustaan
dress code لباس مناسب libaas munaasib
drink n مشروب mashroob; v يشرب yashrab
drinks menu قائمة المشروبات qaa'imat al-
mashroobaat
drive v يقود yaqood
driver's license رخصة قيادة rukhSa qeeyaada
drop (of liquid) قطرة qaTra
drowsiness خمول khumool
dry cleaner محل تنظيف ألبسة maHal tanZeef albisa
dummy [BE] لهاية lahaaya
during خلال khilaal
duty (customs) رسوم rusoom
duty-free goods بضائع معفية من الضرائب biDaa'i'
mu'feeya min aD-Daraa'ib
DVD دي في دي dee fee dee

E

ear أذن udhn
earache ألم في الأذن alam fee il-udhn
early مبكر mubakkir
earrings حلق Halaq
east شرق sharq
easy سهل sahil
eat يأكل ya'kul
economy class درجة سياحية daraja seeyaaHeeya
Egypt مصر muSr
Egyptian مصري muSree
elbow مرفق mirfaq
electric outlet مأخذ كهرباء ma'khadh kahrabaa'
elevator مصعد miS'ad
e-mail بريد إلكتروني bareed iliktroonee
e-mail address عنوان الكتروني 'unwaan iliktroonee

emergency طوارىء Tawaari'
emergency exit مخرج الطوارئ makhraj aT-Tawaari'
empty adj فارغ faarigh
enamel (jewelry) خزف khazaf
end v ينتهي yantahee
engaged خاطب khaaTib
English (language) الانكليزية al-ingleezeeya
engrave ينقش yunqush
enjoy يستمتع yastamata'
enter يدخل yadkhul
entertainment تسلية tasleeya
entrance مدخل madkhal
envelope ظرف Zarf
epileptic مصاب بداء الصرع muSaab bidaa' aS-Sura'
equipment معدات mu'idaat
escalator سلالم كهربائية salaalim kahrabaa'eeya
e-ticket تذكرة الكترونية tadhkarat iliktrooneeya
e-ticket check-in إجراءات السفر للتذاكر الالكترونية
  ijra'aat as-safar lit-tadhaakir al-iliktrooneeya
evening مساء masaa'
excess luggage وزن أمتعة زائد wazn amti'a zaa'id
exchange v يبدل yubaddil
exchange fee رسم الصرف rasm aS-Sarf
exchange rate سعر الصرف si'r aS-Sarf
excursion رحلة riHla
exhausted منهك munhak
exit v يخرج yakhruj; n خروج khurooj
expensive غالي ghaalee
experienced متمرس mutamarras
express سريع saree'
express bus باص سريع baaS saree'
express train قطار سريع qiTaar saree'
extension رقم فرعي raqm far'ee
extra إضافي iDaafee
extra large كبير جداً kabeer jiddan
extract v (tooth) يخلع yakhla'
eye عين 'ayn

F

face وجه wajah
facial n تنظيف الوجه tanZeef al-wajah
family عائلة 'aa'ila
fan (appliance) مروحة marwaHa
far بعيد ba'eed
farm مزرعة mazra'a
far-sighted مصاب بمد النظر muSaab bi-madd an-naZar

fast سريع saree'
fast-food place مطعم للوجبات السريعة maT'am
  lil-wajabaat as-saree'a
fat free خال من الدسم khaal min ad-dasm
father أب ab
fax فاكس faaks
fax number رقم الفاكس raqm al-faaks
fee رسم rasm
feed v (baby) يطعم yuT'im
ferry معدية mu'deeya
fever حرارة مرتفعة Haraara murtafi'a
field حقل Haql
fill out (form) يملأ yimlaa
fill up (tank) يملأ yimlaa
filling (in tooth) حشوة Hashwa
film (camera) فيلم feelm
fine (good) جيد jayyid; (for breaking law) مخالفة
  mukhaalafa
finger إصبع iSba'
fingernail ظفر Zifr
fire حريق Hareeq
fire department الإطفاء al-iTfaa'
fire door مخرج الحريق makhraj al-Hareeq
first أول awal
first class درجة أولى darajat oola
fit (clothing) يقيس yaqees
fitting room غرفة القياس ghurfat al-qeeyaas
fix v يصلح yuSalliH
fixed-price سعر محدد si'r muHaddad
flashlight فلاش flaash
flash photography تصوير بالفلاش taSweer bil-flaash
flat (on vehicle) بنشر bunshur
flight رحلة جوية riHla jaweeya
floor (underfoot) أرض arD
florist محل الزهور maHal az-zuhoor
flower زهرة zahra
folk music الموسيقى الشعبية al-mooseeqa ash-
  sha'abeeya
food طعام Ta'aam
food processor فرامة faraama
foot قدم qadam
football [BE] كرة القدم kurrat al-qadam
for لـ li-
forecast توقعات الطقس tawqu'aat aT-Taqs
forest غابة ghaaba
fork شوكة shawka

form (to fill in) استمارة istimaara
formula (for baby) طعام للرضع Ta'aam lir-raDa'
fort حصن HiSn
fountain نافورة naafoora
free مجاني majaanee
freezer فريزر freezir
friend صديق Sadeeq
from من min
frying pan مقلاة miqlaah
full-service خدمة كاملة khidma kaamila

G

game لعبة lu'ba
garage جراج garaaj
garbage bag كيس قمامة kees qamaama
gas بنزين binzeen
gas station محطة البنزين maHaTat al-binzeen
gate (at airport) بوابة bawaaba
gel جل jil
generic drug دواء بدون علامة تجارية dawaa'
    bidooni 'alaama tijaareeya
get off (a train/bus/subway) ينزل yanzil
gift هدية hadeeya
gift shop محل الهدايا التذكارية maHal al-hadaayaa
    at-tidhkaareeya
girl بنت bint
girlfriend صاحبة SaaHiba
give يعطي ya'Tee
give way [BE] أعط أحقية الطريق a'aT aHaqeeyat
    aT-Tareeq
glass (for drink) كأس ka's; (material) زجاج zujaaj
glasses نظارات naZaaraat
go يذهب yadh-hab
gold ذهب dhahab
golf جولف golf
golf club مضارب غولف maDaarib golf
golf course أرض الغولف arD al-golf
good جيد jayyid
goodbye مع السلامة ma' as-salaama
good afternoon مساء الخير masaa' al-khayr
good evening مساء الخير masaa' al-khayr
good morning صباح الخير SabaaH al-khayr
gram غرام gram
grandchild حفيد Hafeed
grandparent جد jadd
gray رمادي ramaadee

green أخضر akhDar
grocery store محل الخضار maHal al-khuDaar
groundcloth حصيرة HaSeera
ground floor الطابق الأرضي aT-Taabiq al-arDee
ground-floor room غرفة في الطابق الأرضي ghurfa fee
    iT-Taabiq al-arDee
groundsheet [BE] حصيرة HaSeera
group مجموعة mujmoo'a
guide دليل daleel
guide (book) كتاب عن المكان kitaab 'an al-makaan
guide dog كلب إرشاد العميان kalb irshaad al-'umyaan
Gulf (Persian) الخليج العربي al-khaleej al-'arabee
gym جيمنازيوم jeemnaaziyoom
gynecologist طبيب نسائي Tabeeb nisaa'ee

H

hair شعر sha'r
hairbrush فرشاة الشعر furshaat ash-sha'r
haircut قصة شعر qaSSa sha'r
hair dryer مجفف شعر mujaffif sha'r
hair salon صالون كوافير Saaloon koowaafeer
hairspray مثبت الشعر muthabbit ash-sha'r
hairstylist كوافير koowaafeer
half نصف nusf
half-kilo نصف كيلو nusf-kilo
hammer مطرقة miTraqa
hand يد yad
handbag [BE] حقيبة يد Haqeeba yad
hand luggage [BE] حقيبة يد Haqeeba yad
handicapped معاق mu'aq
handicapped-accessible خاص للمعاقين khaaS
    lil-mu'aqeen
happen يحصل yaHSal
happy سعيد sa'eed
hat قبعة qub'a
hay fever حمى القش Hummi il-qash
head رأس ra's
headache صداع Sudaa'
headphones سماعات samaa'aat
health صحة SiHHa
health food store محل الأطعمة الصحية maHal
    al-aT'imat aS-SiHHeeya
hearing impaired سمعه ضعيف sam'i Da'eef
heart قلب qalb
heart condition قصور في القلب quSoor fee il-qalb
heat الحر al-Hurr

heater سخان sakhaan
heating [BE] تدفئة tadfi'a
hello السلام عليكم as-salaam 'alaykum
helmet خوذة khoodha
help n مساعدة musaa'ada
here هنا huna
hi مرحبا marHaban
high عالي 'aalee
high blood pressure ضغط دم مرتفع DaghuT damm murtafi'
highchair كرسي عالي kursee 'aalin
highlights [in hair] هاي لايت haay laayt
highway الطريق السريع aT-Tareeq as-saree'
hiking boots جزمة مريحة للمشي jazma mareeHa lil-mashi
hill تل till
hire [BE] يستأجر yasta'jir
hire car [BE] سيارة مستأجرة sayaara musta'jara
hitchhike طلب توصيل Talb tawSeel
hold on (telephone) ينتظر yantaZir
holiday [BE] إجازة ijaaza
horsetrack طريق للخيول Tareeq lil-khuyool
hospital مستشفى mustashfa
hostel نزل nuzul
hot ساخن؛ (spicy) حار saakhin; Haar
hotel فندق funduq
hour ساعة saa'a
house بيت bayt
housekeeping services خدمات تنظيف khidmaat tanZeef
how كيف kayf
how much كم الحساب kam al-Hisaab
hug n يعانق yu'aaniq
hungry جائع jaa'i'
hurt v يؤلم yu'alim
husband زوج zawj

I

ibuprofen إيبوبروفين eeboobroofeen
ice machine ماكينة ثلج maakeena thalj
icy يوجد جليد yoojad jileed
ID هوية شخصية haweeya shakhSeeya
ill [BE] مريض mareeD
in في fee
include يشمل yashmal
indoor pool مسبح مسقوف masbaH masqoof

inexpensive غير مكلف ghayr muklif
infected ملتهب multahib
information معلومات ma'loomaat
information desk استعلامات isti'lamaat
insect bite لدغة الحشرات ladghat al-Hasharaat
insect repellent مادة طاردة للحشرات maada Taarida lil-Hasharaat
insert v يدخل yadkhil
inside الداخل ad-daakhil
insomnia أرق araq
instant messenger ماسنجر maasinjar
insulin انسولين insooleen
insurance تأمين ta'meen
insurance card بطاقة تأمين biTaaqat ta'meen
insurance company شركة التأمين shirkat at-ta'meen
interesting مثير للاهتمام mutheer lil-ihtimaam
international دولي doowalee
International Student Card بطاقة طالب دولية biTaaqa Taalib doowaleeya
internet إنترنت internet
internet cafe مقهى إنترنت maqha internet
interpreter مترجم mutarjim
intersection ملتقى الطرق multaqee aT-Turuq
intestine أمعاء am'aa
introduce يقدّم yuqaddim
invoice n محاسبة muHaasaba
Iran إيران eeraan
Iranian إيراني eeraanee
Iraq العراق al-'iraaq
Iraqi عراقي 'iraaqee
Ireland أيرلندا eerlandaa
Irish أيرلندي eerlandee
iron (for clothes) مكواة mikwa
Israel إسرائيل israa'eel

J

jacket جاكيت jaakeet
jar مرطبان marTabaan
jaw فك fakk
jazz موسيقى الجاز mooseeqa al-jaaz
jazz club نادي لموسيقى الجاز naadee li-mooseeqa al-jaaz
jeans بنطلون جينز banTaloon jeenz
jet ski جت سكي jet-ski
jeweler محل المجوهرات maHal al-mujawharaat
jewelry مجوهرات mujawharaat

joint (of body) مفصل mifSal
Jordan الأردن al-urdun
Jordanian أردني urdunee

K

key مفتاح miftaaH
key card كرت المفتاح kart al-miftaaH
key ring حمالة مفاتيح Hamaalat mafaateeH
kiddie pool مسبح للأطفال masbaH lil-aTfaal
kidney (in body) كلية kulya
kilo كيلو kilo
kilogram كيلوغرام kilogram
kilometer كيلومتر kilometer
kiss v يبوس yaboos
kitchen مطبخ maTbakh
kitchen foil [BE] رقائق الألمنيوم raqaa'iq aluminyoom
knee ركبة rukba
knife سكين sikeen
Kuwait الكويت al-kuwayt
Kuwaiti كويتي kuwaytee

L

lace تخريم takhreem
lactose intolerant يتحسس من اللاكتوز yataHasas min al-laaktooz
lake بحيرة buHayra
large كبير kabeer
last آخر aakhar
late (time) متأخر muta'akhir
launderette [BE] محل تنظيف ألبسة بخدمة ذاتية maHal tanZeef albisa bi-khidma dhaateeya
laundromat محل تنظيف ألبسة بخدمة ذاتية maHal tanZeef albisa bi-khidma dhaateeya
laundry ملابس للغسيل malaabis lil-ghaseel
laundry facility مغسلة maghsala
laundry service خدمة غسيل ملابس khidma ghaseel malaabis
lawyer محامي muHaamee
leather جلد jild
leave v (deposit) يترك yatruk; (go away) يغادر yughaadir; (airplane) تغادر tughaadir
Lebanese لبناني lubnaanee
Lebanon لبنان lubnaan
left (direction) يسار yasaar
leg ساق saaq
lens عدسة 'adasa

less أقل aqal
lesson درس dars
letter رسالة risaala
library مكتبة maktaba
Libya ليبيا leebeeyaa
Libyan ليبي leebee
life boat قارب النجاة qaarib an-najaa
lifeguard منقذ munqidh
life jacket سترة النجاة sitrat an-najaa
lift [BE] مصعد miS'ad
light فاتح faatiH; n ضوء Daw'; v (cigarette) يشعل yash'al
lightbulb لمبة lamba
lighter ولاعة walaa'a
like v يحب yuHibb
line خط khaT
linen كتان kataan
lip شفة shiffa
liquor store محل المشروبات الكحولية maHal al-mashroobaat al-kuHooleeya
liter ليتر liter
little صغير Sagheer
live يعيش ya'eesh
live music موسيقى حية mooseeqa Haya
liver (in body) كبد kabd
loafers موكاسان mookaasaan
local محلي maHalee
lock n قفل qifl
lock up يقفل yaqful
locker خزانة khazaana
log off يخرج من الإنترنت yakhruj min al-internet
log on يدخل على الإنترنت yadkhul 'ala al-internet
login دخول dukhool
long طويل Taweel
long-sighted [BE] مصاب بمد النظر muSaab bi-madd an-naZar
look v يشوف yashoof
loose (fit) واسع waasi'
lose (something) يفقد yafqud
lost تائه taa'ih
lost and found الأمتعة المفقودة al-amti'at al-mafqooda
lost property [BE] الأمتعة المفقودة al-amti'at al-mafqooda
lotion غسول ghasool
love n محبة maHabba; v (someone) يحب yuHibb
low منخفض munkhafiD

low blood pressure ضغط دم منخفض DaghuT damm munkhafiD

luggage أمتعة amti'a

luggage cart عربات الأمتعة arabaat al-amti'a

luggage locker خزائن الأمتعة khazaa'in al-amti'a

luggage trolley [BE] عربات الأمتعة 'arabaat al-amti'a

lunch غذاء ghadhaa'

lung رئة ri'a

luxury car سيارة فخمة sayaara fakhma

M

magazine مجلة majalla

magnificent جميل جداً jameel jiddan

mail n بريد bareed

mailbox صندوق البريد Sundooq al-bareed

mall مركز تجاري markaz tijaaree

man رجل rajul

manager مدير mudeer

manicure منيكور maneekoor

manual (car) بغيار عادي bi-ghiyar 'aadee

map خريطة khareeTa

market سوق sooq

married متزوج mutazawwij

mass (in church) قداس qudaas

massage مساج masaaj

match (game) لعبة lu'ba

matches كبريت kibreet

meal وجبة wajba

mean v يعني ya'nee

measuring cup فنجان للعيار finjaan lil-'ayaar

measuring spoon ملعقة للعيار mil'aqa lil-'ayaar

mechanic ميكانيكي meekaaneekee

medication دواء dawaa'

medicine دواء dawaa'

medium (size) متوسط mutawassiT

meet v يلتقي yaltaqee

meeting اجتماع ijtimaa'

meeting room قاعة اجتماعات qaa'at ijtimaa'aat

membership card بطاقة عضوية biTaaqa 'uDweeya

memory card كرت ذاكرة kart dhaakira

mend [BE] يصلح yuSalliH

menu قائمة الطعام qaa'imat aT-Ta'aam

menu of the day طبق اليوم Tabaq al-yawm

merge يدخل في السير yadkhul fee is-sayr

message رسالة risaala

microwave مايكروويف maykroowayif

microwaveable مناسب للمايكروويف munaasib lil-meekroowayif

midday [BE] منتصف النهار muntaSif an-nahaar

midnight منتصف الليل muntaSif al-layl

mileage المسافة المقطوعة al-masaafat al-maqToo'a

mini-bar ميني بار meenee baar

minimum age أدنى adna

minute دقيقة daqeeqa

missing مفقود mafqood

mistake خطأ khaTaa'

mobile home بيت متنقل bayt mutanaqqal

mobile phone [BE] هاتف نقال haatif naqaal

moment لحظة laHza

money مال maal

month شهر shahr

mop ممسحة mimsaHa

moped دراجة بمحرك daraaja bi-muHarrik

more أكثر akthar

morning صباح SabaaH

Moroccan مغربي maghribee

Morocco المغرب al-maghrib

mosque جامع jaami'

mother أم umm

motion sickness دوار السفر dawaar as-safar

motorboat زورق zawraq

motorcycle دراجة نارية daraaja naareeya

motorway [BE] الطريق السريع aT-Tareeq as-saree'

mountain جبل jabal

mountain bike دراجة جبلية daraaja jabaleeya

mousse (hair) موس moos

mouth فم famm

movie فيلم feelm

movie theater صالة سينما Saala seenimaa

mugging سلب Salb

muscle عضلة 'aDla

museum متحف matHaf

music موسيقا mooseeqa

music store محل سيديات maHal al-mooseeqa

Muslim مسلم muslim

N

nail file مبرد للأظافر mibrad lil-aZaafir

nail salon صالون تجميل Saloon tajmeel

name اسم ism

napkin منديل للمائدة mandeel lil-maa'ida

nappy [BE] حفاضات HifaaDaat

nationality جنسية jinseeya
nature preserve محمية طبيعية maHmeeya Tabee'eeya
nauseous يشعر بغثيان yash'ur bi-ghathayaan
near قريب qareeb
near-sighted مصاب بقصر النظر muSaab bi-qaSr an-naZar
neck رقبة ruqba
necklace عقد 'uqd
newspaper جريدة jareeda
next تالي taalee
nice جميل jameel
night مساء masaa
nightclub نادي ليلي naadee laylee
no لا la
non-alcoholic بدون كحول bi-dooni kuHool
non-smoking لغير المدخنين li-ghayr al-mudakhineen
noon منتصف النهار muntaSif an-nahaar
north شمال shimaal
nose أنف anf
not ليس laysa
nothing لا شيء la shay
notify يخبر yukhbir
now الآن al-aan
number رقم raqm
nurse ممرض mumarriD

O

off (light, TV etc) إيقاف eeqaaf
office مكتب maktab
office hours أوقات العمل awqaat al-'amal
off-licence [BE] محل المشروبات الكحولية maHal al-mashroobaat al-kuHooleeya
oil زيت zayt
OK حسناً Hasanan
old قديم qadeem
old town المدينة القديمة al-madeenat al-qadeema
Oman عمان 'omaan
Omani عماني 'omaanee
on (light, TV etc) تشغيل tashgheel
once مرة marra
one واحد waaHid
one-way ذهاب dhihaab
only فقط faqaT
open v يفتح yaftaH; adj مفتوح maftooH
opposite مقابل muqaabil
optician محل نظارات maHal naZaaraat

orange (color) برتقالي burtuqaalee
orchestra أوركسترا oorkistraa
order v يطلب yaTlub
outdoor pool مسبح masbaH
outside في الخارج fee il-khaarij
overheated ساخن أكثر من اللازم saakhin akthar min al-laazim
overlook (scenic place) إطلالة iTlaala
overnight طوال الليل Tawaal al-layl
oxygen treatment علاج بالأوكسجين 'ilaaj bil-awksijeen

P

p.m. بعد الظهر ba'ad aZ-Zuhr
pacifier لهاية lahaaya
package صندوق Sundooq
paddling pool [BE] مسبح أطفال masbaH aTfaal
pain ألم alam
pajamas بيجامة beejaama
palace قصر qaSr
Palestine فلسطين filisTeen
Palestinian فلسطيني filisTeenee
pants بنطلون banTaloon
pantyhose كولون kooloon
paper ورق waraq
paper towel ورقة مناشف manaashif warqeeya
paracetamol [BE] سيتامول seetaamool
park n حديقة عامة Hadeeqa 'aama; v (car) يصف yaSaff
parking موقف mawqif
parking garage موقف جراج mawqif garaaj
parking lot موقف سيارات mawqif sayaaraat
parking meter عداد الموقف 'adaad al-mawqif
part (for car) جزء juz'
part-time دوام جزئي dawaam juz'ee
passenger مسافر musaafir
passport جواز سفر jawaaz safar
passport control مراقبة جوازات السفر muraaqaba jawaazaat as-safar
password كلمة مرور kalima muroor
pastry shop محل حلويات maHal Hilweeyaat
patch يرقى yuraqi
path ممر mamar
pay v يدفع yadfa'
pay phone هاتف عام haatif 'aam
peak n قمة qimma
pearl لؤلؤ loo'loo'
pedestrian crossing [BE] عبور مشاة 'uboor mushaa

pedestrian crosswalk عبور مشاة 'uboor mushaa
pediatrician طبيب أطفال Tabeeb aTfaal
pedicure بديكور bideekoor
pen قلم qalam
penicillin بنسلين penicillin
penis عضو ذكري aDoo dhikree
perfume عطر uTr
period (menstruation) عادة شهرية 'aada shahreeya;
  (of time) مدة mudda
petite صغير جدا Sagheer jiddan
petrol [BE] بنزين binzeen
petrol station [BE] محطة البنزين maHaTat al-binzeen
pewter قصدير qaSdeer
pharmacy صيدلية Saydleeya
phone n تلفون tilifoon; v يتصل yattaSil
phone call اتصال هاتفي ittiSaal haatifee
phone card بطاقة تلفونية biTaaqa tilifooneeya
phone number رقم تلفون raqm tilifoon
photocopy نسخة nuskha
photograph صورة Soora
picnic area منطقة النزهات manTaqat an-nuz-haat
piece قطعة qiT'a
Pill (contraceptive) حبوب منع الحمل Huboob
  mana' al-Haml
pillow مخدة mikhadda
PIN الرقم السري ar-raqm as-sirree
pink زهري zahree
plan خطة khuTTa
plane طائرة Taa'ira
plastic wrap غلاف نايلون ghilaaf naayloon
plate صحن SaHn
platform رصيف raSeef; (at station) [BE] خط khaT
platinum بلاتين blaateen
play n (in theater) مسرحية masraHeeya; v يلعب
  yal'ab
playground ملعب mal'ab
playpen مكان محاط بالشباك للعب makaan muHaaT
  bish-shubaak lil-la'ab
please من فضلك min faDlak
plunger غاطس ghaaTis
point v يشير yusheer
poison سم sam
police الشرطة ash-shurTa
police report تقرير الشرطة taqreer ash-shurTa
police station مركز الشرطة markaz ash-shurTa
pond بركة baraka

pool مسبح masbaH
pop music موسيقى البوب mooseeqa al-pop
post [BE] بريد bareed
postbox [BE] صندوق البريد Sundooq al-bareed
postcard كرت بوستال kart boostaal
post office البريد al-bareed
pot وعاء للطبخ wi'aa' liT-Tabkh
pottery إناء فخاري inaa' fakhaaree
pound (weight) رطل raTl; (sterling) جنيه استرليني
  gunay istirleenee
pregnant حامل Haamil
prepaid مسبق الدفع musabaq ad-dafa'
prescription وصفة طبية waSfa Tibeeya
press (clothes) يكبس yikbis
price سعر si'r
print v يطبع yaTba'
problem مشكلة mushkila
produce store محل الخضار maHal al-khuDaar
pull v يسحب yis-Hab
purple بنفسجي banafsajee
purse حقيبة يد Haqeeba yad
push v يدفع yadfa'
pushchair [BE] عربة أطفال arabat aTfaal
pyjamas [BE] بيجامة beejaama

Q

Qatar قطر qaTar
Qatari قطري qaTaree
quality نوعية naw'eeya
question سؤال su'aal
quiet هادئ haadi'

R

racetrack مضمار السباق miDmaar as-sibaaq
racket (sports) مضرب miDrab
railway station [BE] محطة القطار maHaTat al-qiTaar
rain n مطر maTar
raincoat معطف للمطر mi'Taf lil-maTar
rainy ممطر mumTir
rap (music) موسيقى الراب mooseeqa ar-rap
rape n اغتصاب ightiSaab
rash n طفح جلدي TafH jildee
razor موس الحلاقة moos al-Hilaaqa
razor blade شفرات الحلاقة shafaraat al-Hilaaqa
reach (person) يجد yajid
ready جاهز jaahiz

real أصلي aSlee
receipt إيصال eeSaal
receive v يستقبل yastaqbil
reception استقبال istiqbaal
recharge v يشحن yash-Han
recommend ينصح yanSaH
recycling إعادة التصنيع i'aadat at-taSnee'
red أحمر aHmar
refrigerator ثلاجة thallaaja
refund n استرداد النقود istirdaad an-nuqood
region منطقة manTaqa
regular عادي 'aadee
relationship (personal) علاقة 'ilaaqa
rent v يستأجر yasta'jir
rental car سيارة مستأجرة sayaara musta'jara
repair v يصلح yuSalliH
report v يبلغ عن yuballigh 'an
reservation حجز Hajz
reserve v يحجز yaHjuz
restaurant مطعم maT'am
restroom تواليت toowaleet
retired متقاعد mutaqaa'id
return v يعود ذهاب وعودة dhihaab; n [BE] وعودة wa-'awda
rib ضلع Dala'
right (correct) صحيح SaHeeH; (direction) يمين yameen
right of way أحقية الطريق aHqeeyat aT-Tareeq
ring n خاتم khaatim
river نهر nahr
road طريق Tareeq
road map خريطة طرق khareeTa Turuq
romantic رومانسي roomaansee
room غرفة ghurfa
room key مفتاح الغرفة miftaaH al-ghurfa
room service خدمة غرف khidma ghuruf
rotary دوار dawaar
round (in game) جولة jawla
roundabout [BE] دوار dawaar
round-trip ذهاب وعودة dhihaab wa-'awda
round-trip ticket تذكرة ذهاب وعودة tadhkara dhihaab wa-'awda
route طريق Tareeq
rubbish [BE] قمامة qamaama
rubbish bag [BE] أكياس قمامة akyaas qamaama
ruins آثار aathaar

S

sad حزين Hazeen
safe n خزينة khazeena; (not dangerous) آمن aamin; (not in danger) بأمان bi-amaan
sales tax ضريبة Dareeba
salty مالح maaliH
same نفس nafs
sandals صندل Sandal
sanitary napkin فوط نسائية fuwaT nisaa'eeya
sanitary pad [BE] فوط نسائية fuwaT nisaa'eeya
Saudi سعودي sa'oodee
Saudi Arabia السعودية as-sa'oodeeya
sauna ساونا saawnaa
save حفظ HafZ
savings account حساب المدخرات Hisaab al-mudakharaat
scanner ماسحة maasiHa
scarf لفاح lifaaH
schedule n جدول مواعيد jadwal mawaa'eed
school مدرسة madrassa
scissors مقص miqaSS
sea بحر baHr
seat مقعد maq'ad
security أمن aman
see يشوف yashoof
sell يبيع yabee'
self-service خدمة ذاتية khidma dhaateeya
seminar ندوة nadwa
send يرسل yursil
senior citizen مسنين musneen
separate منفصل munfaSil
serious خطير khaTeer
service خدمة khidma; (in church) صلاة Salaat
shampoo شامبو shamboo
shaving cream كريم للحلاقة kreem lil-Hilaaqa
sheet شراشف sharaashif
shirt قميص qameeS
shoe store محل الأحذية maHal al-aHdheeya
shoes أحذية aHdheeya
shopping تسوق tasawooq
shopping area منطقة التسوق manTaqat at-tasawooq
shopping centre [BE] سوق تجاري markaz at-tijaaree
shopping mall سوق تجاري markaz at-tijaaree
short قصير qaSeer
shorts شورت shoort
short-sighted [BE] مصاب بقصر النظر muSaab

bi-qaSr an-naZar
shoulder كتف katif
show v يري yuree
shower دُش doosh
shrine مزار mazaar
sick مريض mareeD
sightseeing tour جولة لزيارة المعالم jawla li-ziyaarat al-ma'aalim
sign v يوقع yuwaqi'a
silk حرير Hareer
silver فضة fiDDa
single عازب 'aazib
single bed سرير مفرد sareer mufrad
single room غرفة مفردة ghurfa mufrada
single ticket [BE] تذكرة ذهاب tadhkara dihaab
sister أخت ukht
sit يجلس yajlis
size قياس qeeyaas
skin جلد jild
skirt تنورة tanoora
sleeping bag حقيبة للنوم Haqeeba lin-nawm
slice شريحة shareeHa
slippers شبشب shibshib
slow بطيء baTee'
slowly بي بطء bi-buT'
small صغير Sagheer
smoking للمدخنين lil-mudakhineen
snack bar مطعم للوجبات الخفيفة maT'am lil-wajabaat al-khafeefa
sneakers أحذية رياضية aHdheeya reeyaaDeeya
snorkeling equipment شنركل snorkel
snowy يتساقط الثلج yatasaaqaT ath-thalj
soap صابون Saaboon
soccer كرة القدم kurrat al-qadam
socks جرابات juraabaat
sold out خلصت التذاكر khalaSat at-tadhaakir
sore throat ألم الحلق alam al-Halq
sorry (apology) آسف aasif
south جنوب janoob
souvenir هدايا تذكارية hadaayaa tidhkaareeya
souvenir store محل الهدايا التذكارية maHal al-hadaayaa at-tidhkaareeya
spa سبا spa
sparkling water مياه غازية miyaah ghaazeeya
spatula ملعقة مسطحة mil'aqa musaTaHa
speak يتكلم yatakallam

special خاص khaaS
specialist n أخصائي akhSaa'ee
spicy حار Haar
spine عمود فقري 'amood faqree
sporting goods store محل الأدوات الرياضية maHal al-adawaat ar-reeyaaDeeya
sprain n الالتواء في المفصل iltiwaa' fee il-mifSal
sprained ملتوي multawee
stadium ملعب mal'ab
stairs درج daraj
stamp n طابع Taabi'
start v يبدأ yabda'
station محطة maHaTat
station wagon سيارة بوكس sayaara books
stay v ينزل yanzil
steal يسرق yasriq
steep شديد الانحدار shadeed al-inHidaar
sterling silver فضة fiDDa
stolen مسروق masrooq
stomach معدة mi'da
stomachache ألم في المعدة alam fee il-mi'da
stool (bowel movement) براز biraaz
stop v يقف yaqif; n (on bus route) موقف mawqif
store directory دليل المحلات التجارية daleel al-maHaalat at-tijaareeya
stove فرن furn
straight مستقيم mustaqeem
straight ahead على طول 'ala Tool
strange غريب ghareeb
stream جدول jadwal
street شارع shaari'
stroller عربة أطفال 'arabat aTfaal
student طالب Taalib
study v يدرس yadrus
stunning مذهل mudh-hil
subway مترو الأنفاق metro al-anfaaq
subway station محطة مترو الأنفاق maHaTat metro al-anfaaq
Sudan السودان as-soodaan
Sudanese سوداني soodaanee
suit (clothing) طقم Taqm
suitable مناسب munaasib
suitcase حقيبة Haqeeba
sun شمس shams
sunblock واقي شمسي waaqee shamsee

sunburn حروق شمسية Hurooq shamseeya
sunglasses نظارات شمسية naZaaraat shamseeya
sunny مشمس mushmis
sunscreen واقي شمسي waaqee shamsee
sunstroke ضربة شمس Darba shams
super (fuel) ممتاز mumtaaz
supermarket سوبر ماركت soobir maarkit
surcharge أجرة إضافية ujrat iDaafeeya
surfboard لوح لركوب الأمواج looH li-rukoob al-amwaaj
surgical spirit [BE] كحول طبي kuHool Tibbee
swallow v يبتلع yabtala'
sweater كنزة صوف kanza Soof
sweatshirt كنزة رياضة kanza reeyaaDa
sweet حلو Hiloo
sweets [BE] سكاكر sakaakir
swim v يسبح yasbaH
swimsuit مايوه maayooh
Syria سوريا sooriyaa
Syrian سوري sooree

T

table طاولة Taawila
tablet حبة Habba
take v يأخذ ya'khudh
take off (shoes) يخلع yikhla'
tampon سدادات قطنية للسيدات sadadaat quTneeya
  lis-sayyidaat
taste v يتذوق yatadhawwaq
taxi تاكسي taaksee
tea شاي shaay
team فريق fareeq
teaspoon ملعقة صغيرة mil'aqa Sagheera
telephone تلفون tilifoon
temple (religious) معبد ma'bad
temporary مؤقت mu'aqat
tennis التنس at-tinnis
tennis court ملاعب تنس malaa'ib tinnis
tent خيمة khayma
tent peg أوتاد الخيمة awtaad al-khayma
tent pole عمود الخيمة 'amood al-khayma
terminal (airport) تيرمنال teerminaal
terrible فظيع faZee'
text v يبعث اس ام اس yab'ath SMS; n اس ام اس SMS
thank you شكراً shukran
that ذلك dhaalik
theater مسرح masraH

theft سرقة sirqa
there هناك hunaak
thief لص liSS
thigh فخذ fakhdh
thirsty عطشان 'aTshaan
this هذا haadha
throat حلق Halq
thunderstorm عاصفة رعدية 'aaSifa ra'deeya
ticket تذكرة tadhkara
ticket office مكتب التذاكر maktab at-tadhaakir
tie n كرافيت kraafeet
tight (fit) ضيق Dayyiq
tights [BE] كولون kooloon
time وقت waqt
timetable [BE] جدول مواعيد jadwal mawaa'eed
tire دولاب doolaab
tired تعبان ta'baan
tissue مناديل ورقية manaadeel warqeeya
to إلى ila
today اليوم al-yawm
toe إصبع القدم iSba' al-qadam
toenail ظفر إصبع القدم Zifr iSba' al-qadam
toilet [BE] تواليت toowaleet
toilet paper ورق تواليت waraq toowaaleet
toll road طريق برسم مرور Tareeq bi-rasm muroor
tomorrow غداً ghadan
tonight الليلة al-layla
too (also) أيضاً ayDaan; (excessively) أكثر من اللازم
  akthar min al-laazim
tooth سن sinn
toothache ألم في الأسنان alam fee il-asnaan
toothbrush فرشاة أسنان furshaat asnaan
toothpaste معجون أسنان ma'joon asnaan
torch [BE] بيل beel
total (amount) مُجمل mujmal
tour جولة jawla
tourist سائح saa'iH
tourist information office مكتب الاستعلامات
  السياحة maktab al-isti'laamaat as-seeyaaHeeya
tow truck شاحنة قاطرة shaaHina qaaTira
towel منشفة minshafa
tower برج burj
town مدينة madeena
town hall البلدية al-baladeeya
town map خريطة المدينة khareeTat al-madeena
town square ساحة المدينة saaHat al-madeena

toy لعبة أطفال lu'bat aTfaal
toy store محل ألعاب الأطفال maHal al'aab al-aTfaal
track (for trains) خط khaT
traditional تقليدي taqleedee
traffic circle دوار dawaar
traffic light إشارة مرور ishaarat muroor
trail ممر mamar
trailer عربة مقطورة 'araba maqToora
train n قطار qiTaar
train station محطة قطار maHaTat qiTaar
transfer v (traveling) يبدل yubaddil
translate يترجم yutarjim
trash قمامة qamaama
travel agency مكتب سياحة وسفر maktab seeyaaHa wa safar
travelers check شيك سياحي sheek seeyaaHee
traveller's cheque [BE] شيك سياحي sheek seeyaaHee
travel sickness [BE] دوار السفر dawaar as-safar
tree شجرة shajara
trim (haircut) تطريف شعر taTreef sha'r
trip رحلة riHla
trolley [BE] عربة 'araba
trousers [BE] بنطلون banTaloon
T-shirt تي شيرت tee sheert
tumble dry يعصر في الغسالة yu'aSar fee il-ghasaala
Tunisia تونس toonis
Tunisian تونسي toonisee
turn off (light) يطفئ yaTfa'
turn on (light) يشعل yash'al
TV تلفزيون tilifizyoon
tyre [BE] دولاب doolaab

U

ugly بشع bashi'
umbrella مظلة maZalla
underground [BE] مترو الأنفاق metro al-anfaaq
underground station [BE] محطة مترو الأنفاق maHaTat metro al-anfaaq
underpants [BE] سروال داخلي sirwaal daakhilee
understand يفهم yafham
underwear ملابس داخلية malaabis dakhileeya
United Kingdom بريطانيا breeTaaneeya
United States أمريكا amreekaa
unleaded بدون رصاص bi-dooni raSaaS
unlimited mileage بأميال غير محدودة bi-amyaal ghayr maHdooda

urgent مستعجل musta'jil
urine بول bool
use v يستخدم yastakhdim
username اسم المستخدم ism al-mustakhdim
utensil أدوات الطبخ adawaat aT-Tabkh

V

vacation إجازة ijaaza
vacuum cleaner مكنسة كهربائية miknasa kahrabaa'eeya
vagina مهبل mahbil
vaginal infection التهاب مهبلي iltihaab mahbalee
valley وادي waadee
value n قيمة qeema
van فان van
VAT [BE] ضريبة Dareeba
vegan لا يأكل المنتجات الحيوانية la ya'kul al-muntajaat al-Haywaaneeya
vegetarian نباتي nabaatee
vehicle registration تسجيل سيارة tasjeel sayaara
vending machine ماكينة بيع maakeena bay'
very جداً jiddan
viewpoint [BE] إطلالة iTlaala
visit v يزور yazoor
visiting hours مواعيد الزيارة mawaa'eed az-ziyaara
visually impaired نظره ضعيف naZarhu Da'eef
volleyball كرة الطائرة kurrat aT-Taa'ira
vomiting يتقيأ yataqayaa'

W

wait v ينتظر yantaZar
waiter غرسون gharsoon
waiting room غرفة انتظار ghurfat intiZaar
waitress آنسة aanisa
wake (person) يوقظ yawqiZ
wake-up call مكالمة إيقاظ mukaalamat eeqaaZ
walk n نزهة nuz-ha
walking route طرق السير Turuq as-sayr
wallet محفظة miHfaZa
warm دافئ daafi'; v يسخن yusakhin
wash v يغسل yughassal
washing machine غسالة الملابس ghasaalat al-malaabis
washing-up liquid [BE] سائل للجلي saa'il lil-jallee
watch n ساعة يد saa'a yad
water ماء maa'

waterfall شلال shalaal
water skis ألواح للتزلج على الماء al-waaH lit-tazaHluq 'ala al-maa'
weather طقس Taqs
week أسبوع usboo'
weekend عطلة نهاية الأسبوع 'uTla nihaayat al-usboo'
weekly أسبوعي usboo'ee
well-rested مرتاح murtaaH
west غرب gharb
what ماذا maadha
wheelchair كرسي المقعدين kursee al-muq'adeen
wheelchair ramp منحدر خاص لكرسي المقعدين munHadir khaaS li-kursee al-muq'adeen
when متى mata
where أين ayn
where to إلى أين ila ayn
which أي ay
white أبيض abyaD
white gold ذهب أبيض dhahab abyaD
who من man
widowed أرمل armal
wife زوجة zawja
window نافذة naafidha
window seat مقعد على النافذة maq'ad 'ala an-naafidha
windsurfer لوح شراعي looH shiraa'ee
wine list قائمة النبيذ qaa'imat an-nabeedh
wireless internet إنترنت لاسلكي internet lasilkee

wireless internet service خدمة إنترنت لاسلكي khidmat internet lasilkee
with مع ma'
withdraw يسحب yas-Hab
without بدون bi-doon
woman امرأة imraa'a
wool صوف Soof
work v يعمل ya'mal
wrist معصم mi'Sam
write (down) يكتب yuktub

Y

year سنة sana
yellow أصفر aSfar
yellow gold ذهب أصفر dhahab aSfar
Yemen اليمن al-yaman
Yemeni يمني yamanee
yes نعم na'am
yesterday البارحة al-baariHa
yield (in traffic) أعط أحقية الطريق a'aT aHaqeeyat aT-Tareeq
yogurt لبن laban
young شاب shaab
you're welcome عفواً afwaan
youth hostel بيت شباب bayt shabaab

Z

zoo حديقة الحيوانات Hadeeqat al-Hayawaanaat

ARABIC-ENGLISH

A

a'aT aHaqeeyat aT-Tareeq أعط أحقية الطريق yield (give way BE)
a'maal أعمال business
'aada shahreeya عادة شهرية period (menstruation)
'aadee عادي regular
'aa'ila عائلة family
aakhar آخر another
aakhir آخر last
'aalee عالي high
aamin آمن safe (not dangerous)
aanisa آنسة waitress

aasif آسف sorry
'aaSifa ra'deeya عاصفة رعدية thunderstorm
aathaar آثار ruin
aathaar jaanibeeya آثار جانبية side effect
'aazib عازب single
ab أب father
abyaD أبيض white
'adaad al-mawqif عداد الموقف parking meter
'adasa عدسة lens
'adasa laaSiqa عدسة لاصقة contact lens
adawaat aT-Tbkh أدوات الطبخ utensil
'adeem an-nuk-ha عديم النكهة bland (food)

adna 'umr أدنى عمر minimum age
aDla عضلة muscle
aDu dhikree عضو ذكري penis
afDal أفضل better
'afwaan عفواً that's ok
aHaqeeyat aT-Tareeq أحقية الطريق right of way
aHdheeya أحذية shoes
aHdheeya reeyaaDeeya أحذية رياضية sneakers
ahlaan wa sahlaan أهلاً و سهلاً you're welcome
aHmar أحمر red
aHsan أحسن best
AIDS أيدز aydz
akh أخ brother
akhDar أخضر green
akhSaa'ee أخصائي specialist *n*
akthar أكثر more
akthar min al-laazim أكثر من اللازم excessively, too
akyaas qamaama أكياس قمامة garbage bag [bin bag BE]
'ala Tool على طول straight ahead
al-aan الآن now
alam ألم pain
alam al-Halq ألم الحلق sore throat
alam fee il-asnaan ألم في الأسنان toothache
alam fee il-mi'da ألم في المعدة stomach ache
alam fee iS-Sadr ألم في الصدر chest pain
alam fee il-udhn ألم في الأذن earache
alam fee iZ-Zuhr ألم في الظهر backache
al-amti'a al-mafqooda الأمتعة المفقودة lost and found [lost property BE]
'alaykum عليكم hello
al-baariHa البارحة yesterday
alghee الغي cancel
al-khaleej al-'arabee الخليج العربي Gulf (Persian)
al-layla الليلة tonight
al-maas ألماس diamond
al-waaH lit-tazaHluq 'ala al-maa' ألواح للتزحلق على الماء water ski
al-wuSool الوصول arrivals (airport)
al-yawm اليوم today
aman أمان security
'amood faqree عمود فقري spine
'amood lil-khayma عمود الخيمة tent pole
amreekaa أمريكا United States
amreekaanee أمريكي American
amti'a أمتعة luggage

anf أنف nose
aqal أقل less
'araba عربة cart [trolley BE]
'araba maqToora عربة مقطورة trailer
'arabat al-amti'a عربات الأمتعة luggage cart [trolley BE]
'arabat aTfaal عربة أطفال stroller [pushchair BE]
'arabee عربي Arab, Arabic; **al-'arabeeya** العربية Arabic (language)
araq أرق insomnia
'arboon عربون deposit
arD أرض floor
arD al-golf أرض الغولف golf course
'arD baalayh عرض باليه ballet
'arD oobiraa عرض أوبرا opera
armal أرمل widowed
aSam أصم deaf
asbireen أسبرين aspirin
aSeer عصير juice
aSfar أصفر yellow
'ashaa عشاء dinner
aSlee أصلي real
aswad أسود black
'aTshaan عطشان thirsty
awal أول first
awqaat al-'amal أوقات العمل office hours
awqaat al-'amal أوقات العمل business hours
awtaad al-khayma أوتاد الخيمة tent peg
awtoomaateekee أوتوماتيكي automatic
ay أي which
ay shay أي شيء anything
ayDan أيضاً too (also)
ayn أين where
'ayn عين eye
aZm عظم bone
azraq أزرق blue

B

baab باب door
ba'ad بعد after
ba'ad aZ-Zuhr بعد الظهر afternoon, p.m.
baar بار bar
baarid بارد cold *adj*
baarid qaleelan بارد قليلاً cool (temperature)
baaS باص bus
baaS saree' باص سريع express bus

ba'eed بعيد far
baHr بحر sea
baHraynee بحريني Bahraini; al-baHrayn البحرين Bahrain
baladeeya البلدية town hall
balsam بلسم conditioner
banafsajee بنفسجي purple
bank بنك bank
banTaloon بنطلون pants [trousers BE]
banTaloon jeenz بنطلون جينز jeans
baraka بركة pond
bareed بريد mail n [post BE], post office
bareed iliktroonee بريد إلكتروني e-mail
baysbool بيسبول baseball
bashi' بشع ugly
baTaareeya بطارية battery
baTaneeya بطانية blanket
baTee' بطيء slow
bawaaba بوابة gate (at airport)
bawabaat as-safar بوابات السفر departure gate
bayj بيج beige
bayt بيت house
bayt mutanaqil بيت متنقل mobile home
bayt shabaab بيت شباب youth hostel
bideekoor بديكور pedicure
beejaama بيجامة pajamas [pyjamas BE]
beel بيل flashlight [torch BE]
binzeen بنزين gas [petrol BE]
bi-amaan بأمان safe, not in danger
bi-buT' ببطء slowly
biDaa'i' lil-i'laan 'anhaa بضائع للإعلان عنها goods to declare
biDaa'i' mu'afeeya min aD-Daraa'ib بضائع معفية من الضرائب duty-free goods
bi-doon بدون without
bi-dooni raSaaS بدون رصاص unleaded
bi-ittijah markaz al-madeena باتجاه مركز المدينة downtown
bi-ghiyar 'aadee بغيار عادي manual (car)
bi-munfaridih بمفرده alone
penicillin (binisileen) بنسلين penicillin
bint بنت girl
biraaz براز stool (bowel movement)
biTaaqa بطاقة card
biTaaqa tilifooneeya بطاقة تلفونية phone card
biTaaqa 'uDweeya بطاقة عضوية membership card

biTaaqat i'timaan بطاقة ائتمان credit card
biTaaqat Su'ood بطاقة صعود boarding pass
biTaaqa Taalib doowaleeya بطاقة طالب دولية International Student Card
biTaaqa ta'meen بطاقة تأمين insurance card
blaateen بلاتين platinum
blooza بلوزة blouse
bool بول urine
breeTaanee بريطاني British adj
breeTaaneeyaa بريطانيا United Kingdom
broosh بروش brooch
buHayra بحيرة lake
bunnee بني brown
bunshur بنشر flat (on vehicle)
burj برج tower
burtuqaal برتقال orange (fruit)
burtuqaalee برتقالي orange (color)

D

daafi' دافئ warm
daakhil داخل inside
Dala' ضلع rib
daleel دليل guide
daleel al-maHalaat at-tijaareeya دليل المحلات التجارية store directory
Damaadaat ضمادات bandage
damm دم blood
daqeeqa دقيقة minute
daraaja دراجة bicycle
daraaja bi-muHarik دراجة بمحرك moped
daraaja jabaleeya دراجة جبلية mountain bike
daraaja naareeya دراجة نارية motorcycle
daraj دَرَج stair
darajat oola درجة أولى first class
daraja seeyaaHeeya درجة سياحية economy class
darajaat درجات degrees (temperature)
darajat al-a'maal درجة الأعمال business class
Darbat shams ضربة شمس sunstroke
Dareeba ضريبة sales tax [VAT BE]
dars درس lesson
dawaa' دواء medication, medicine
dawaa' bidooni 'alaama tijaareeya دواء بدون علامة تجارية generic drug
dawaam juz'ee دوام جزئي part-time
dawaar دوار traffic circle [roundabout BE]
dawaar as-safar دوار السفر motion [travel BE] sickness

daw' ضوء light n
Dayyiq ضيق tight (fit)
dee fee dee دي في دي DVD
deezil ديزل diesel
dhaalik ذلك that
dhahab ذهب gold
dhahab abyaD ذهب أبيض white gold
dhahab aSfar ذهب أصفر yellow gold
dhihaab ذهاب one-way (single BE) (ticket)
dhihaab wa-'awda ذهاب وعودة round-trip (return n BE) (ticket)
dhiraa' ذراع arm
dijeetaal ديجيتال digital
doolaab دولاب tire (tyre BE)
doolaar دولار dollar
doosh دش shower
doowalee دولي international
duf'a musabbaqa دفعة مسبقة cash advance
DaghuT damm munkhafiD ضغط دم منخفض low blood pressure
DaghuT damm murtafi' ضغط دم مرتفع high blood pressure
dukhool دخول login
dumya دمية doll
duzeena دزينة dozen

E

'eed meelaad عيد ميلاد birthday
eedaa' إيداع deposit (at bank)
eeqaaf إيقاف off
eeraan إيران Iran
eeraanee إيراني Iranian
eerlandaa أيرلندا Ireland
eerlandee أيرلندي Irish
eeSaal إيصال receipt

F

faarigh فارغ empty adj
faatiH فاتح light
faHam فحم charcoal
fakhdh فخذ thigh
fakk فك jaw
famm فم mouth
faqaT فقط only
faraama فرامة food processor
faraamil فرامل brake

fareeq فريق team
fataaHat an-nabeedh فتاحة النبيذ corkscrew
fataaHat zujajaat فتاحة زجاجات bottle opener
faaks فاكس fax
faZee' فظيع terrible
fee في in
fee il-khaarij في الخارج outside
feelm فيلم movie, film (camera)
fee iS-SubH في الصبح a.m.
fiDDa فضة silver
filisTeen فلسطين Palestine
filisTeenee فلسطيني Palestinian
finjaan فنجان cup
finjaan lil-'ayaar فنجان للعيار measuring cup
fireezir فريزر freezer
fitreenaa فترينا display case
flaash فلاش flashlight (torch BE)
funduq فندق hotel
furn فرن stove
furn mukhayyam فرن مخيم camping stove
furshaat ash-sha'r فرشاة الشعر hairbrush
furshaat asnaan فرشاة أسنان toothbrush
fustaan فستان dress (woman's)
fuToor فطور breakfast
fuwaT nisaa'eeya فوط نسائية sanitary napkins (sanitary pads BE)

G

garaaj جراج garage
ghaaba غابة forest
ghaalee غالي expensive
ghaamik غامق dark
ghaaz aT-Tabkh غاز الطبخ cooking gas
ghadan غداً tomorrow
ghadhaa' غذاء lunch
gharb غرب west
ghareeb غريب strange
gharsoon غرسون waiter
ghasaalat al-malaabis غسالة الملابس washing machine
ghasaalat aS-SuHoon غسالة الصحون dishwasher
ghasool غسول lotion
ghayr mashghool غير مشغول available
ghayr muklif غير مكلف inexpensive
gram (ghraam) غرام gram
ghurfa غرفة room

ghurfa fee iT-Taabiq al-arDee غرفة في الطابق الأرضي ground-floor room

ghurfa mufrada غرفة مفردة single room

ghurfa muzdawwaja غرفة مزدوجة double room

ghurfat intiZaar غرفة انتظار waiting room

ghurfa nawm غرفة نوم dormitory

ghurfa qeeyaas غرفة قياس fitting room

ghurfa Ta'aam غرفة طعام dining room

golf الغولف golf

gunay istirleenee جنيه استرليني pound (sterling)

H

haadi' هادئ quiet

Haadith حادث accident

Haadith iSTidaam حادث اصطدام crash n (in car)

Haamil حامل pregnant

Haar حار hot (spicy)

haatif 'aam هاتف عام pay phone

haatif naqaal هاتف نقال cell [mobile BE] phone

haay laayt هاي لايت highlights (in hair)

Habba حبة tablet

hadaayaa tidhkaareeya هدايا تذكارية souvenir

Hadeeqa 'aama حديقة عامة park n

Hadeeqat al-Hayawanaat حديقة الحيوانات zoo

Hadeeqat an-nabaataat حديقة النباتات botanical garden

hadeeya هدية gift

Hafeed حفيد grandchild

Hafla mooseeqeeya حفلة موسيقية concert

HafZ حفظ save

Hajz حجز reservation

Halaal حلال halal

Halaaq rijaalee حلاق رجالي barber

Halaq حلق earrings

Halq حلق throat

Hamaalat mafaateeH حمالة مفاتيح key ring

Hamaalat Sadr حمالة صدر bra

Hamaam حمام bathroom

Haqeeba حقيبة suitcase

Haqeeba lin-nawm حقيبة للنوم sleeping bag

Haqeeba yad حقيبة يد carry-on [hand luggage BE]

Haqeeba yad حقيبة يد purse [handbag BE]

Haqeeba Zuhr حقيبة ظهر backpack

Haql حقل field

Haraara murtafi'a حرارة مرتفعة fever

Hareeq حريق fire

Hareer حرير silk

Harq حرق burn n

Hasanan حسناً OK

haSeera حصيرة groundcloth [groundsheet BE]

Hasharaat حشرات bug

Hashwa حشوة filling (in tooth)

haweeya shakhSeeya هوية شخصية ID

Haywaan حيوان animal

haadha هذا this

Hazeen حزين sad

Hiloo حلو sweet

Hizaam حزام belt

HifaaDaat حفاضات diaper [nappy BE]

Hisaab حساب account; bill; check (in restaurant)

Hisaab al-jaaree حساب الجاري checking account

Hisaab al-mudakharaat حساب المدخرات savings account

HiSn حصن fort

Huboob mana' al-Haml حبوب منع الحمل Pill (contraceptive)

Hummi il-qash حمى القش hay fever

huna هنا here

hunaak هناك there

Hurayraat حريرات calorie

Hurooq shamseeya حروق شمسية sunburn

Hurr حر heat

I

i'aadat at-taSnee' إعادة التصنيع recycling

i'tidaa' اعتداء attack

i'timaan ائتمان credit

ibreeq إبريق carafe

iDaafee إضافي extra

ightiSaab اغتصاب rape n

iHtiqaan احتقان congestion

ijaaza إجازة vacation [holiday BE]

ijra'aat as-safar إجراءات السفر check-in

ijra'aat as-safar lit-tadhaakir al-iliktrooneeya إجراءات السفر للتذاكر الالكترونية e-ticket check-in

ijtimaa' اجتماع meeting

ila إلى to

ila ayn إلى أين where to

'ilaaj aroomaatee علاج أروماتي aromatherapy

'ilaaj bil-ibar علاج بالإبر acupuncture

'ilaaj bil-awksijeen علاج بالأوكسجين oxygen treatment

'ilaaqa علاقة relationship (personal)

'ilka علكة chewing gum
iltihaab mafaaSil التهاب مفاصل arthritis
iltihaab mahbalee التهاب مهبلي vaginal infection
iltiwaa' fee il-mifSal التواء في المفصل sprain n
im'aa أمعاء intestine
imraa'a امرأة woman
inaa' fakharee إناء فخاري pottery
ingleezee إنكليزي English; al-ingleezeeya الانكليزية English (language)
insooleen انسولين insulin
internet إنترنت internet
internet lasilkee إنترنت لاسلكي wireless internet
iqtiHaam اقتحام break-in
'iraaqee عراقي Iraqi; al-'iraaq العراق Iraq
iSba' إصبع finger
iSba' al-qadam إصبع القدم toe
is-haal إسهال diarrhea
ishaarat al-muroor إشارة المرور traffic light
ism اسم name
ism al-mustakhdim اسم المستخدم username
israa'eel إسرائيل Israel
isti'laamaat استعلامات information (telephone) [directory enquiries BE], information desk
istilaam al-Haqaa'ib استلام الحقائب baggage claim
istiqbaal استقبال reception
istimaara استمارة form (to fill in)
istimaara muTaalaba استمارة مطالبة claim form
istirdaad an-nuqood استرداد النقود refund n
iTfaa' إطفاء fire department
itijaah اتجاه direction
iTlaala إطلالة overlook (scenic place) [viewpoint BE]
ittiSaal اتصال connection
ittiSaal haatifee اتصال هاتفي phone call

J

jaa'i' جائع hungry
jaahiz جاهز ready
jaakeet جاكيت jacket
jaami' جامع mosque
jabal جبل mountain
jadd جد grandparent
jadwal جدول stream
jadwal mawaa'eed جدول مواعيد schedule [timetable BE]
jameel جميل beautiful, nice, cute
jameel jiddan جميل جداً magnificent

janoob جنوب south
jareeda جريدة newspaper
jawaaz safar جواز سفر passport
jayyid جيد fine, good
jadhaab جذاب attractive (person)
jazaa'iree جزائري Algerian; al-jazaa'ir الجزائر Algeria
jazma جزمة boot
jazma mareeHa lil-mashi جزمة مريحة للمشي hiking boot
jeenz جينز denim
jet-ski جت سكي jet ski
jiddan جداً very
jil جل gel
jild جلد leather, skin
jeemnaaziyoom جيمنازيوم gym
jinseeya جنسية nationality
jisr جسر bridge
jisr munkhafiD جسر منخفض low bridge
jawla جولة round (in game), tour
jawla bil-baaS جولة بالباص bus tour
jawla li-ziyaarat al-ma'aalim جولة لزيارة المعالم sightseeing tour
jumruk جمرك customs
juraabaat جرابات sock
jurH جرح cut n
juz' جزء part (for car)

K

kaabeena كابينة cabin
kaaHil كاحل ankle
kaameeraa كاميرا camera
kaameeraa dijeetaal كاميرا دجيتال digital camera
kaash كاش cash
kabd كبد liver (in body)
kabeer كبير big
kabeer jiddan كبير جداً extra large
kahf كهف cave
kalb irshaad al-'umyaan كلب إرشاد العميان guide dog
kalimat al-muroor كلمة مرور password
kam al-Hisaab كم الحساب how much
kanadaa كندا Canada
kanadee كندي Canadian
kaneesa كنيسة church
kanza reeyaaDa كنزة رياضة sweatshirt
kanza Soof كنزة صوف sweater
kart al-a'maal كرت الأعمال business card

kart al-miftaH كرت المفتاح key card
kart boostaal كرت بوستال postcard
kart dhaakira كرت ذاكرة memory card
kartoona كرتونة carton
ka's كأس glass (for drink)
kataan كتان linen
katif كتف shoulder
kayf كيف how
kazeenoo كازينو casino
kees كيس bag
kees qamaama كيس قمامة garbage bag [bin bag BE]
khaal min ad-dasm خال من الدسم fat free
khaaS خاص special
khaaS lil-mu'aaqeen خاص للمعاقين
    handicapped-accessible
khaaTib خاطب engaged
khaatim خاتم ring n
khalaaT خلاط blender
khalaSat at-tadhaakir خلصت التذاكر sold out
khalf خلف behind
khareeTa خريطة map
khareeTat al-madeena خريطة المدينة town map
khareeTa Turuq خريطة طرق road map
khaT خط line
khaTaa' خطأ mistake
khaTeer خطير dangerous, serious
khaT خط track (for train) [platform BE]
khayma خيمة tent
khazaana خزانة locker
khazaf خزف enamel
khazeena خزينة safe n
khazaa'in al-amti'a خزائن الأمتعة luggage locker
khidma kaamila خدمة كاملة full-service
khidma dhateeya خدمة ذاتية self-service
khidmaat tanZeef خدمات تنظيف housekeeping
    service
khidma ghaseel malaabis خدمة غسيل ملابس
    laundry service
khidma ghuruf خدمة غرف room service
khidmat internet lasilkee خدمة إنترنت لاسلكي
    wireless internet service
khidma خدمة service
khilaal خلال during
khoodha خوذة helmet
khumool خمول drowsiness
khurooj خروج exit

khuTooT jaweeya خطوط جوية airline
khuTTa خطة plan
kibreet كبريت matches
kilo كيلو kilo
kilogram كيلوغرام kilogram
kilometer كيلومتر kilometer
kitaab كتاب book
kitaab 'an al-makaan كتاب عن المكان guide book
kooloon كولون pantyhose [tights BE]
kooloonyaa كولونيا cologne
koorn fliks كورن فلكس cereal
koowaafeer كوافير hairstylist
kraafeet كرافيت tie n
kreem lil-Hilaaqa كريم للحلاقة shaving cream
kreem mu'qim كريم معقم antiseptic cream
kreestaal كريستال crystal
kuHool Tibbee كحول طبي rubbing alcohol [surgical
    spirit BE]
kulfat al-mukaalamat 'ala al-muttaSil كلفة المكالمة
    على المتصل call collect
kulya كلية kidney (in body)
kumbyootir كومبيوتر computer
kurrat al-qadam كرة القدم soccer [football BE]
kurrat as-silla كرة السلة basketball
kurrat aT-Taa'ira كرة الطائرة volleyball
kursee كرسي chair
kursee 'aalin كرسي عالي highchair
kursee al-muq'adeen كرسي المقعدين wheelchair
kursee khaaS lil-aTfaal كرسي خاص للأطفال
    child's seat
kursee lish-shaaTee' كرسي للشاطئ deck chair
kuwaytee كويتي Kuwaiti; al-kuwayt الكويت Kuwait

L

la لا no
la shay لا شيء nothing
laaHiqan لاحقاً later
ladghat al-Hasharaat لدغة الحشرات insect bite
ladheedh لذيذ delicious
laHaam لحام butcher
lahaaya لهاية pacifier [dummy BE]
laHZa لحظة moment
lamba لمبة lightbulb
lawaazim Tabkh لوازم طبخ cooking facility
laysa ليس not
leebee ليبي Libyan

leebeeyaa ليبيا Libya
li-لـ, ل for
libaas munaasib لباس مناسب dress code
lifaaH لفاح scarf
li-ghayr al-mudakhineen لغير المدخنين non-smoking
lil-isti'maal marra waaHida للاستعمال مرة واحدة disposable
lil-mudakhineen للمدخنين smoking
lisaan لسان tongue
liSS لص thief
liter لتر liter
looH li-rukoob al-amwaaj لوح لركوب الأمواج surfboard
looH shiraa'ee لوح شراعي windsurfer
loo'loo' لؤلؤ pearl
lu'ba لعبة game
lu'ba لعبة match (game)
lu'bat aTfaal لعبة أطفال toy
lubnaan لبنان Lebanon
lubnaanee لبناني Lebanese

M

ma' مع with
ma' as-salaama مع السلامة goodbye
maa' ماء water
maa' saakhin ماء ساخن hot water
maadha ماذا what
ma'joon asnaan معجون أسنان toothpaste
ma'bad معبد temple (religious)
maada Taarida lil-Hasharaat مادة طاردة للحشرات insect repellent
maakeena bay' ماكينة بيع vending machine
maakeena thalj ماكينة ثلج ice machine
ma'akhadh kahrabaa' مأخذ كهرباء electric outlet
maal مال money
maaliH مالح salty
ma'loomaat معلومات information
maasiHa ماسحة scanner
maayoh مايوه swimsuit
mabna مبنى building
maDaarib golf مضارب غولف golf club
madeena مدينة town
madeena qadeema مدينة قديمة old town
madeenat al-malaahee مدينة الملاهي amusement park
madkhal مدخل access, entrance
madrasa مدرسة school
mafqood مفقود missing

maftooH مفتوح open adj
maghribee مغربي Moroccan; al-maghrib المغرب Morocco
maghsala مغسلة laundry facility
maHaarim liT-Tifl محارم للطفل baby wipe
maHabba محبة love n
maHal al'aab al-aTfaal محل ألعاب الأطفال toy store
maHal al-adawaat ar-reeyaaDeeya محل الأدوات الرياضية sporting goods store
maHal al-aHdheeya محل الأحذية shoe store
maHal al-anteekaat محل الأنتيكات antiques store
maHal al-aT'imat as-siHHeeya محل الأطعمة الصحية health food store
maHal al-hadaayaa at-tidhkaareeya محل الهدايا التذكارية gift shop, souvenir store
maHal al-kaameeraat محل الكاميرات camera store
maHal al-khuDaar محل الخضار grocery store
maHal al-malaabis محل الملابس clothing store
maHal al-mashroobaat al-kuHooleeya محل المشروبات الكحولية liquor store [off-licence BE]
maHal al-mooseeqa محل سيدات music store
maHal al-mujawharaat محل المجوهرات jeweler
maHal az-zuhoor محل الزهور florist
maHal al-Halaweeyaat محل الحلويات pastry shop
maHal naZaaraat محل نظارات optician
maHal tanZeef albisa محل تنظيف ألبسة dry cleaner
maHal tanZeef albisa bi-khidma dhaateeya محل تنظيف ألبسة بخدمة ذاتية laundromat [launderette BE]
maHal tijaaree محل تجاري department store
maHalee محلي domestic
maHalee محلي local
maHaTat محطة station (railroad)
maHaTat al-baaS محطة الباص bus station
maHaTat al-binzeen محطة البنزين gas [petrol BE] station
maHaTat al-qiTaar محطة القطار train station
maHaTat metro al-anfaaq محطة مترو الأنفاق subway [underground BE] station
mahbil مهبل vagina
maHlool lil-'adasaat al-laaSiqa محلول للعدسات اللاصقة contact lens solution
maHmeeya Tabee'eeya محمية طبيعية nature preserve
majaanee مجاني free
majalla مجلة magazine
majmoo'a مجموعة group

makaan muHaaT bish-shubaak li-la'ab مكان محاط بالشباك للعب playpen

makaan mujahhaz li-istiqbaal al-mu'aaqeen مكان مجهز لاستقبال المعاقين handicapped- [disabled-BE] accessible

makhbaz مخبز bakery

makhraj مخرج exit

makhraj al-Hareeq مخرج الحريق fire door

makhraj aT-Tawaari' مخرج الطوارئ emergency exit

maksoor مكسور broken

maktab مكتب office

maktab al-isti'laamaat as-seeyaaHeeya مكتب الاستعلامات السياحية tourist information office

maktab at-tadhaakir مكتب التذاكر ticket office

maktab seeyaaHa wa safar مكتب سياحة و سفر travel agency

maktab tabdeel al-'umlaat مكتب تبديل العملات currency exchange office

maktaba مكتبة bookstore, library

malaabis ملابس clothes

malaabis dakhileeya ملابس داخلية underwear

malaabis lil-ghaseel ملابس للغسيل laundry (clothes)

malaa'ib at-tinnis ملاعب تنس tennis court

mal'ab ملعب playground, stadium

mamar ممر path, trail

(bayD) mamzooj بيض ممزوج scrambled

man من who

manaadeel warqeeya مناديل ورقية tissue, paper towel

manadeel siHHeeya مناديل صحية sanitary [pad BE] napkin

mandeel lil-maa'ida منديل للمائدة napkin

maneekoor منيكور manicure

manTaqa منطقة region

manTaqat an-nuz-haat منطقة النزهات picnic area

manTaqat at-tasawooq منطقة التسوق shopping area

maq'ad مقعد seat

maq'ad 'ala al-mamsha مقعد على الممشى aisle seat

maq'ad 'ala an-naafidha مقعد على النافذة window seat

maq'ad sayaara مقعد سيارة car seat

maqha مقهى cafe, coffee shop

maqha internet مقهى إنترنت internet cafe

marra مرة once

mareeD مريض sick [ill BE]

mareeD bir-raboo مريض بالربو asthmatic

mareeD bis-sukaree مريض بالسكري diabetic

marHaban مرحبا hi

marham مرهم cream (ointment)

markaz al-a'maal مركز الأعمال business center

markaz al-madeena مركز المدينة downtown area

markaz ash-shurTa مركز الشرطة police station

markaz at-tijaaree مركز تجاري shopping mall [centre BE]

marTabaan مرطبان jar

marwaHa مروحة fan [appliance]

masaa' مساء evening, night

masaa' al-khayr مساء الخير good afternoon, good evening

masaaj مساج massage

masbaH مسبح pool

masbaH lil-aTfaal مسبح للأطفال kiddie [paddling BE] pool

masbaH masqoof مسبح مسقوف indoor pool

mashghool مشغول busy

mashroob مشروب drink n

(qaa'imat al-) mashroobaat قائمة المشروبات drinks menu

masmooH مسموح allowed

masraH مسرح theater

masraHeeya مسرحية play n (in theater)

masrooq مسروق stolen

mata متى when

maTaar مطار airport

maT'am مطعم restaurant

maTar مطر rain n

maTbakh مطبخ kitchen

mathaana مثانة bladder

mat-Haf متحف museum

mawaad tanZeef مواد تنظيف cleaning supplies

mawaa'eed az-ziyaara مواعيد الزيارة visiting hours

maw'id موعد appointment

mawqif موقف parking, stop (on bus route)

mawqif al-baaS موقف الباص bus stop

mawqif as-sayaaraat موقف السيارات parking lot [car park BE]

mazaar مزار shrine

maZalla مظلة umbrella

mazra'a مزرعة farm

meekaaneekee ميكانيكي mechanic

meekroowayf مايكروويف microwave

metro al-anfaaq مترو الأنفاق subway [underground BE]

mi'da معدة stomach

mi'Sam معصم wrist
mi'Taf معطف coat
mi'Taf lil-maTar معطف للمطر raincoat
mibrad lil-aZaafir مبرد للأظافر nail file
miDmaar as-sibaaq مضمار السباق racetrack
miDrab مضرب racket (sports)
mifSal مفصل joint (of body)
miftaaH مفتاح key
miftaaH al-ghurfa مفتاح الغرفة room key
miHfaZa محفظة wallet
mikhadda مخدة pillow
miknasa مكنسة broom
miknasa kahrabaa'eeya مكنسة كهربائية vacuum
   cleaner
mikwa مكواة iron (for clothes)
mil'aqa ملعقة spoon
mil'aqa lil-'ayaar ملعقة للعيار measuring spoon
mimsaHa ممسحة mop
min من from
min faDlak من فضلك please
minfaakh منفاخ air pump
meenee baar بار ميني mini-bar
minshafa منشفة towel
miqaSS مقص scissors
miqlaah مقلاة frying pan
mirfaq مرفق elbow
miS'ad مصعد elevator (lift BE)
miSfaah مصفاة colander
mishT مشط comb
miTraqa مطرقة hammer
miyaah ghaazeeya مياه غازية sparkling water
miyaah ma'daneeya مياه معدنية still water
mookaasaan موكاسان loafer
moos موس mousse (hair)
moos al-Hilaaqa موس الحلاقة razor
mooseeqa موسيقى music
mooseeqa al-jaaz موسيقى الجاز jazz
mooseeqa al-pop موسيقى البوب pop music
mooseeqa ar-rap موسيقى الراب rap music
mooseeqa ash-sha'abeeya موسيقى شعبية folk music
mooseeqa Haya موسيقى حية live music
mooseeqa klaaseekeeya موسيقى كلاسيكية
   classical music
mu'aaq معاق handicapped [disabled BE]
mu'adeeya معدية ferry
mu'aqat مؤقت temporary

mu'tamar مؤتمر conference
mubakkir مبكر early
mubtadi' مبتدىء beginner
muDaadaat al-Hayawaya مضادات حيوية antibiotics
mudakhan مدخن smoked
mudda مدة period (of time)
mudeer مدير manager
mudh-hil مذهل stunning
mud-hish مدهش amazing
mu'din معدن contagious
mughaadara مغادرة departure
mughaadarat al-funduq مغادرة الفندق check-out
   (from hotel)
mughlaq مغلق closed
muHaamee محامي lawyer
muHaasaba محاسبة invoice n
muHaasib محاسب cashier
muHawwil محوّل adapter
muhd aTfaal مهد أطفال crib [cot BE]
muHlee Sinaa'ee مُحلي صناعي artificial sweetener
mu'idaat معدات equipment
mu'iddaat lil-ghawS معدات الغوص diving equipment
mujaffif sha'r مجفف شعر hair dryer
mujmal مُجمل total
mujawharaat مجوهرات jewelry
mukaalamat eeqaaZ مكالمة إيقاظ wake-up call
mukayyif al-hawaa' مكيف الهواء air conditioner
mukhaalafa مخالفة fine (for breaking law)
mukhayyam مخيم campsite
mulaakama ملاكمة boxing
multahib ملتهب infected
multaqee aT-Turuq ملتقى الطرق intersection
multawee ملتوي sprained
mumarriD ممرض nurse
mumill ممل boring
mumtaaz ممتاز super (fuel)
mumTir ممطر rainy
munaasib مناسب suitable
munaasib lil-meekroowayif مناسب للمايكرويف
   microwaveable
munaZZif منظف detergent
munfaSil منفصل separate
munHadir منحدر cliff
munHadir khaaS li-kursee al-muq'adeen منحدر
خاص لكرسي المُقعدين wheelchair ramp
munkhafiD منخفض low

munhak منهك exhausted
munqidh منقذ lifeguard
muntaSif al-layl منتصف الليل midnight
muntaSif an-nahaar منتصف النهار noon
muqaabil مقابل opposite
muraaqaba jawaazaat as-safar مراقبة جوازات السفر passport control
murabeeyat aTfaal مربية أطفال babysitter
murtaaH مرتاح well-rested
musaa'ada مساعدة help n
muSaab bidaa' aS-Sura مصاب بداء الصرع epileptic
muSaab bi-imsaak مصاب بإمساك constipated
muSaab bi-fuqr ad-damm مصاب بفقر الدم anemic
muSaab bi-madd an-naZar مصاب بمد النظر far-[long- BE] sighted
muSaab bi-qasr an-naZar مصاب بقصر النظر near-[short- BE] sighted
musaafir مسافر passenger
musabaq ad-dafa' مسبق الدفع prepaid
mushkila مشكلة problem
mushmis مشمس sunny
musinn مسن senior citizen
muslim مسلم Muslim
muSr مصر Egypt
muSree مصري Egyptian
musta'jil مستعجل urgent
mustaqeem مستقيم straight
mustashaar مستشار consultant
mustashfa مستشفى hospital
muta'akhir متأخر late (time)
muTallaq مطلق divorced
mutamarras متمرس experienced
mutaqaa'id متقاعد retired
mutarjim مترجم interpreter
mutawassiT متوسط medium (size)
mutazawwij متزوج married
muthabbit ash-sha'r مثبت الشعر hairspray
mutheer lil-ihtimaam مثير للاهتمام interesting
muzeel ar-raa'iHa مزيل الرائحة deodorant

N

naadee نادي club
naadee laylee نادي ليلي nightclub
naadee lir-raqS نادي للرقص dance club
naadee li-mooseeqa al-jaaz نادي لموسيقى الجاز jazz club

naafidha نافذة window
naafoora نافورة fountain
na'am نعم yes
nabaatee نباتي vegetarian
nadwa ندوة seminar
nafs نفس same
nahr نهر river
naw'eeya نوعية quality
naZaaraat نظارات (eye)glasses
naZaaraat shamseeya نظارات شمسية sunglasses
naZarhu Da'eef نظره ضعيف visually impaired
naZeef نظيف clean adj
nuHaas نحاس copper
nuSf نصف half
nuSf-kilo نصف كيلو half-kilo
nuskha نسخة photocopy
nuz-ha نزهة walk n
nuzul نزل hostel

O

oorkistraa أوركسترا orchestra

Q

qaa'at ijtimaa'aat قاعة اجتماعات meeting room
qaa'at al-al'aab قاعة الألعاب arcade
qaa'at al-Haflaat al-mooseeqeeya قاعة الحفلات الموسيقية concert hall
qaa'at al-mu'tamaraat قاعة المؤتمرات convention hall
qaa'imat an-nabeedh قائمة النبيذ wine list
qaa'imat aT-Ta'aam قائمة الطعام menu
qaa'imat Ta'aam lil-aTfaal قائمة طعام للأطفال children's menu
qaa'imat Ta'aam ma' al-as'aar قائمة طعام مع الأسعار fixed-price menu
qaarib قارب boat
qaarib an-najaah قارب النجاة life boat
qabl قبل before
qadam قدم foot
qadeem قديم old
qahwa قهوة coffee
qal'a قلعة castle
qalb قلب heart
qamaama قمامة trash [rubbish BE]
qameeS قميص shirt
qareeb قريب close, near
qaSdeer قصدير pewter

qaSeer قصير short
qaSr قصر palace
qaSSa sha'r قصة شعر haircut
qaTar قطر Qatar
qaTaree قطري Qatari
qaTra قطرة drop (of liquid)
qeema قيمة value n
qeeyaas قياس size
qifl قفل lock n
qimma قمة peak n
qiT'a قطعة piece
qiT'a naqdeeya قطعة نقدية coin
qiTaar قطار train n
qiTaar saree' قطار سريع express train
qub'a قبعة hat
qudaas قداس mass (in church)
qunSuleeya قنصلية consulate
quSoor fee il-qalb قصور في القلب heart condition
quTn قطن cotton

R

radee' رديء bad
raDee' رضيع baby
rajul رجل man
rakheeS رخيص cheap
ramaadee رمادي gray
ramz al-balad رمز البلد country code
ramz al-manTaqa رمز المنطقة area code
raqaa'iq aluminyoom رقائق الألمنيوم aluminum [kitchen BE] foil
raqm رقم number
raqm al-faaks رقم الفاكس fax number
raqm far'ee رقم فرعي extension
raqm as-sirree رقم السري PIN
raqm tilifoon رقم تلفون phone number
raqS رقص dancing
ra's رأس head
raSeef رصيف platform
rashH رشح cold n (illness)
rasm رسم fee
rasm ad-dukhool رسم الدخول admission (to museum etc)
rasm al-khidma رسم الخدمة cover charge
rasm aS-Sarf رسم الصرف exchange fee
ratl رطل pound (weight)
ri'a رئة lung

riDaa'a رضّاعة baby bottle
ridfayn ردفين buttock
riHla رحلة excursion, trip
riHla bil-qaarib رحلة بالقارب boat trip
riHla jaweeya رحلة جوية flight
risaala رسالة letter
risaala رسالة message
rool رول roll
roomaansee رومانسي romantic
rukba ركبة knee
rukhSa qeeyaada رخصة قيادة driver's license
rukoob ad-daraaja ركوب الدراجة cycling
ruqba رقبة neck
rusoom jumrukeeya رسوم جمركية duty (customs)

S

saa'a Haa'iTeeya ساعة حائطية clock
saa'a ساعة hour
saa'a yad ساعة يد watch n
Saaboon صابون soap
saaHat al-madeena ساحة المدينة town square
SaaHib صاحب boyfriend
SaaHiba صاحبة girlfriend
saa'iH سائح tourist
saa'il li-ghaseel aS-SuHoon سائل لغسيل الصحون dishwashing [washing-up BE] liquid
saakhin ساخن hot
Saala seenimaa صالة سينما movie theater
Saaloon koowaafeer صالون كوافير hair salon
saawnaa ساونا sauna
saaq ساق leg
SabaaH صباح morning
SabaaH al-khayr صباح الخير good morning
Sabee صبي boy
Sabgha صبغة color
sadaadaat quTneeya lis-sayyidaat سدادات قطنية للسيدات tampon
Sadeeq صديق friend
Sadr صدر chest
sa'eed سعيد happy
Saff صف class (in school)
Sagheer صغير little, small
saHab min al-Hisaab سحب من الحساب debit
SaHeeH صحيح right, correct
sahil سهل easy
SaHn صحن dish, plate

SaHraa' صحراء desert
sakaakir سكاكر candy [sweets BE]
saakhun akthar min al-laazim ساخن أكثر من اللازم overheated
salaalim kahrabaa'eeya سلالم كهربائية escalator
Salaat صلاة service (in church)
salb سلب mugging
Saloon tajmeel صالون تجميل nail salon
samaa'aat سماعات headphone
sami' Da'eef سمع ضعيف hearing impaired
sam سم poison
sana سنة year
Sandal صندل sandals
centimeter (santimitir) سنتمتر centimeter
sa'oodee سعودي Saudi; as-sa'oodeeya السعودية Saudi Arabia
Saraaf aalee صراف آلي ATM
saree' سريع fast
sareer سرير bed
sareer aTfaal سرير أطفال crib [cot BE]
sareer mufrad سرير مفرد single bed
sareer muzdawwaj سرير مزدوج double bed
sareer qaabil liT-Tawwi سرير قابل للطوي cot [campbed BE]
sawt a'la صوت أعلى louder
sayaara سيارة car
sayaara fakhma سيارة فخمة luxury car
sayaara musta'jara سيارة مستأجرة rental [hire BE] car
sayaarat al-is'aaf سيارة الإسعاف ambulance
Saydleeya صيدلية pharmacy [chemist BE]
see dee سي دي CD
seegaar سيجار cigar
silseeyoos سلسيوس Celsius
shaab شاب young
shaaHina qaaTira شاحنة قاطرة tow truck
sha'r شعر hair
shaari' شارع street
shaaTee' شاطئ beach
shadeed al-inHidaar شديد الانحدار steep
shafaraat al-Hilaaqa شفرات الحلاقة razor blade
shahaada شهادة certificate
shahr شهر month
shajara شجرة tree
shakwa شكوى complaint
shalaal شلال waterfall
shama' khaT al-beekeenee شمع خط البيكيني bikini wax

shaamboo شامبو shampoo
shams شمس sun
sharaashif شراشف sheet
shareeHa شريحة slice
sharq شرق east
shawka شوكة fork
sheek شيك check (payment) [cheque BE]
sheek seeyaaHee شيك سياحي travelers check [traveller's cheque BE]
shibshib شبشب slipper
shiffa شفة lip
shimaal شمال north
shiqqa شقة apartment
shirka ta'meen شركة تأمين insurance company
shoort شورت shorts
shukran شكراً thank you
shurTa الشرطة police
siHHa صحة health
sijaa'ir سجائر cigarette
sikeen سكين knife
silla سلة basket
sinn سن tooth
si'r سعر price, charge (cost)
si'r aS-Sarf سعر الصرف exchange rate
si'r muHaddad سعر محدد fixed-price
sirqa سرقة theft
sirwaal daakhilee سروال داخلي briefs [underpants BE]
sitrat an-najaah سترة النجاة life jacket
siwaar سوار bracelet
SMS اس ام اس text message
snorkel (shnurkil) شنركل snorkeling equipment
Sooda صودا soda
soodaanee سوداني Sudanese; as-soodaan السودان Sudan
Soof صوف wool
soobir maarkit سوبر ماركت supermarket
sooq سوق market
Soora صورة photograph
sooree سوري Syrian
sooriyaa سوريا Syria
spa (sbaa) سبا spa
su'aal سعال cough n
su'aal سؤال question
Sudaa' صداع headache
Sundooq صندوق package

Sundooq al-bareed صندوق البريد mailbox [postbox BE]
Su'ub صعب difficult
Suwwar dijeetaal صور دجيتال digital photo

T

Ta'aam طعام food
Ta'aam lir-raDa طعام للرضع baby food, formula
Ta'aam mujammad طعام محمد frozen food
ta'Tul تعطل breakdown
ta'baan تعبان tired
Taabi'a طابع stamp n
Taabiq al-arDee طابق أرضي ground floor
taa'ih تائه lost
Taa'ira طائرة airplane
ta'jeer as-sayaaraat تأجير السيارات car rental [hire BE]
taalee تالي next
Taalib طالب student
taalif تالف damaged
ta'meen تأمين insurance
ta'reekh تاريخ date (on calendar)
ta'Tal تعطل broke down
Taawila طاولة table
Tabaq al-yawm طبق اليوم menu of the day
aTbaaq iDaafee أطباق إضافية side dish
tabdeel al-'umlaat تبديل العملات currency exchange
tabdeel Taa'ira تبديل طائرة connection (in travel)
Tabeeb طبيب doctor
Tabeeb asnaan طبيب أسنان dentist
Tabeeb aTfaal طبيب أطفال pediatrician
Tabeeb nisaa'ee طبيب نسائي gynecologist
tadfi'a تدفئة heater [heating BE]
tadhkara تذكرة ticket
tadhkarat iliktrooneeya تذكرة الكترونية e-ticket
tadhkara lil-baaS تذكرة للباص bus ticket
tadhkara dhihaab wa 'awda تذكرة ذهاب و عودة
round-trip [return BE] ticket
TafH jildee طفح جلدي rash n
taHmeeD تحميض develop (film)
taHweela تحويلة detour
takhdeer تخدير anesthesia
takhfeeD تخفيض discount
takhreem تخريم lace
taaksee تاكسي taxi
Talb tawSeel طلب توصيل hitchhike
tanoora تنورة skirt
tanZeef al-wajah تنظيف الوجه facial n

taqleedy تقليدي traditional
Taqm طقم suit (clothing)
taqreer ash-shurTa تقرير الشرطة police report
Taqs طقس weather
Tareeq طريق road, route
Tareeq aakhar طريق آخر alternate route
Tareeq lil-khuyool طريق للخيول horsetrack
Tareeq bi-rasm muroor طريق برسم مرور toll road
Tareeq saree' طريق سريع highway [motorway BE]
tasawooq تسوق shopping
tashanuj تشنج cramp
tashgheel تشغيل on
tasjeel sayaara تسجيل سيارة vehicle registration
tasleeya تسلية entertainment
taSreeH jumrukee تصريح جمركي customs declaration form
taSweer bil-flaash تصوير بالفلاش flash photography
taTreef sha'r تطريف شعر trim (haircut)
Tawaal al-layl طوال الليل overnight
Tawaari' طوارىء emergency
tawqu'aat aT-Taqs توقعات الطقس forecast
Taweel طويل long
Tayr طير bird
tee sheert تي شيرت T-shirt
tilifizyoon تلفزيون TV
tinnis تنس tennis
teerminaal تيرمنال terminal (airport)
thaddee ثدي breast
thalj ثلج ice
thallaaja ثلاجة refrigerator
Tifl طفل child
tilifoon تلفون phone n
till تل hill
toonis تونس Tunisia
toonisee تونسي Tunisian
toowaaleet تواليت restroom [toilet BE]
toowaaleet khaaS lil-mu'aaqeen تواليت خاص للمعاقين disabled restroom [toilet BE]
toowaaleet kimiyaa'ee تواليت كيميائي chemical toilet
tughaadir تغادر leave (airplane)
turaDDi' ترضع breastfeed
Turuq as-sayr طرق السير walking route

U

'uboor mushaa عبور مشاة pedestrian crosswalk [crossing BE]

udhn أذن ear
ujrat iDaafeeya أجرة إضافية surcharge
ukht أخت sister
'ulba علبة box
'umaan عمان Oman
'umaanee عماني Omani
'umla عملة currency
umm أم mother
'umr عمر age
'unwaan عنوان address
'unwaan iliktroonee عنوان الكتروني e-mail address
'uqd عقد necklace
urdunee أردني Jordanian; al-urdun الأردن Jordan
usboo' أسبوع week
usboo'ee أسبوعي weekly
ustraalee أسترالي Australian
ustraaleeyaa أستراليا Australia
'uTla nihaayat al-usboo' عطلة نهاية الأسبوع
    weekend
'uTr عطر perfume
'uTr ba'ad al-Halaaqa عطر بعد الحلاقة aftershave

V

van (faan) فان van

W

waadee وادي valley
waaDiH واضح clear adj
waaHid واحد one
waaqee dhikree واقي ذكري condom
waaqee shamsee واقي شمسي sunblock
waasi' واسع loose (fit)
waHdee وحدي on my own
wajabaat aSghar lil-aTfaal وجبات أصغر للأطفال
    children's portion
wajah وجه face
wajba وجبة meal
wakaala وكالة agency
walaa'a ولاعة lighter (cigarettes)
waqt وقت time
waraq ورق paper
waraq toowaaleet ورق تواليت toilet paper
waSfa Tibeeya وصفة طبية prescription
wazn amti'a zaa'id وزن أمتعة زائد excess luggage
wisikh وسخ dirty

Y

ya'kul يأكل eat
ya'mal يعمل work v
ya'nee يعني mean v
yaaqa mudawwara ياقة مدورة crew neck
yab'ath SMS يبعث اس ام اس text v
yabda يبدأ begin, start v
yabee يبيع sell
yaboos يبوس kiss v
yabtala يبتلع swallow v
yad يد hand
yadfa يدفع pay v
yadh-hab يذهب go
yadkhil يدخل insert v
yadkhul يدخل enter
yadkhul 'ala al-internet يدخل على الإنترنت log on
yadkhul fee is-sayr يدخل في السير merge v
yadrus يدرس study v
ya'eesh يعيش live v
yafham يفهم understand
yafHaS يفحص check v
yafqud يفقد lose (something)
yaftaH يفتح open v
yaghliq يغلق close v
yaghTus يغطس dive v
yaHjuz يحجز reserve v
yaHSal يحصل happen
yajid يجد reach (person)
yajlib يجلب bring
yajlis يجلس sit
yakhla يخلع extract v (tooth)
yakhruj يخرج exit v
yakoon يكون be
ya'lab يلعب play v
yaltaqee يلتقي meet v
yamanee يمني Yemeni; al-yaman اليمن Yemen
yameen يمين right (direction)
yamHi يمحي delete v
yanSaH ينصح recommend
yantahee ينتهي end v
yantaZar ينتظر wait v
yanzif ينزف bleed
yanzil ينزل get off (a train/bus/subway)
yanzil ينزل descend, stay v
ya'ood يعود return v
yaqbal يقبل accept

yaqees يقيس fit v (clothing)
yaqful يقفل lock up
yaqif يقف stop
yaqood يقود drive v
yaqTa' al-ittiSaal يقطع الاتصال disconnect
yaquSS يقص cut v (hair)
yarquS يرقص dance v
yasaar يسار left (direction)
yaSaff يصف park v (car)
yasbaH يسبح swim v
yas-Hab يسحب withdraw, pull
yash'al يشعل light v (cigarette)
yash'al يشعل turn on (light)
yash-Han يشحن recharge v
yashoof يشوف look v
yashoof يشوف see
yashrab يشرب drink v
yashtaree يشتري buy v
yash'ur bi-duwaar يشعر بدوار dizzy
yash'ur bi-ghathayaan يشعر بغثيان nauseous
yaSil يصل arrive
yasriq يسرق steal
yasta'jir يستأجر rent v (hire BE)
yastakhdim يستخدم use v
yastamata' يستمتع enjoy
yastaqbil يستقبل receive v
yata'khar يتأخر delay n
yatadhawwaq يتذوق taste v
yatakallam يتكلم speak
yatanaffas يتنفس breath
yataqaya' يتقأ vomiting
yatasaaqaT ath-thalj يتساقط الثلج snowy
yaTba' يطبع print v
yaTbukh يطبخ cook v
yaTfa' يطفئ turn off (light)
yaTlub يطلب charge v, order
yatruk يترك leave v (deposit)
yattaSil يتصل call (telephone)
yattaSil يتصل contact v, connect, phone
yattaSil laaHiqan يتصل لاحقاً call back
yazoor يزور visit v
yiDghuT يضغط dial v
yimlaa يملأ fill out (form)
yimlaa يملأ fill up (tank)
yawm يوم day
yawqiZ يوقظ wake (person)

yu'Tee يعطي give
yu'aanee min al-Hasaaseeya يعاني من الحساسية allergic
yu'aaniq يعانق hug v
yu'akid يؤكد confirm
yu'lim يؤلم hurt v
yu'aSar fee il-ghasaala يعصر في الغسالة tumble dry
yubaddil يبدل change (money); exchange v; transfer
yuballigh 'an يبلغ عن report v
yughaadir يغادر leave (go away)
yughassal يغسل wash v
yughayir يغير change v
yuHibb يحب like, love v (someone)
yukallif يكلف cost v
yukassir يكسر break (tooth, bone)
yukhayyam يخيم camp v
yukhbir يخبر notify
yuktub يكتب write (down)
yunqush ينقش engrave
yuqaddim يقدم introduce yuraafiq يرافق accompany
yuraqi' يرقع patch
yuree يري show v
yursil يرسل send
yusakhin يسخن warm v
yuSalliH يصلح repair v
yutarjim يترجم translate
yuT'im يطعم feed v (baby)
yuwaqi' يوقع sign v

Z

zaa'idat ad-doodeeya زائدة دودية appendix
zaaweeya زاوية corner
zahra زهرة flower
zahree زهري pink
zameel زميل colleague
Zarf ظرف envelope
zayt زيت oil
zibda زبدة butter
zawj زوج husband
zawja زوجة wife
zawraq زورق motorboat
zubdeeya زبدية bowl
Zuhr ظهر back (of body)
zujaaj زجاج glass (material)
zujaaja زجاجة bottle

INDEX

Berlitz pocket guide

DUBAI

Fifth Edition 2018

Editor: Sian Marsh
Author: Matt Jones
Head of Production: Rebeka Davies
Picture Editor: Tom Smyth
Cartography Update: Carte
Update Production: Apa Digital
Photography Credits: 4Corners Images 1;
Alamy 29, 33, 53; Apa Publications 79; Apa
Publications 15, 16, 19, 31, 76; Chris Bradley/
Apa Publications 5M, 82; Corbis 51, 91; Dubai
Tourism 5MC, 7, 67, 68, 101; Getty Images 5T,
5MC, 21, 23, 104; iStock 4TC, 4TL, 5TC, 5M,
7R, 11, 12, 26, 34, 37, 39, 40, 47, 48, 54, 56,
58, 61, 63, 65, 70, 73, 74, 81, 84, 88, 96, 103,
107, 109; Jumeirah Hotels and Resorts 94;
Kevin Cummins/Apa Publications 6L, 43, 52,
87, 93; Shutterstock 4MC, 4ML, 6R, 44
Cover Picture: Shutterstock

Distribution
UK, Ireland and Europe: Apa Publications
(UK) Ltd; sales@insightguides.com
United States and Canada: Ingram
Publisher Services; ips@ingramcontent.com
Australia and New Zealand: Woodslane;
info@woodslane.com.au
Southeast Asia: Apa Publications (SN) Pte;
singaporeoffice@insightguides.com
Worldwide: Apa Publications (UK) Ltd;
sales@insightguides.com

**Special Sales, Content Licensing
and CoPublishing**
Insight Guides can be purchased in bulk
quantities at discounted prices. We can
create special editions, personalised jackets
and corporate imprints tailored to your
needs. sales@insightguides.com;
www.insightguides.biz

Berlitz®

speaking your language

phrase book & dictionary
phrase book & CD

Available in: Arabic, Brazilian Portuguese*, Burmese*, Cantonese Chinese, Croatian, Czech*, Danish*, Dutch, English, Filipino, Finnish*, French, German, Greek, Hebrew*, Hindi*, Hungarian*, Indonesian, Italian, Japanese, Korean, Latin American Spanish, Malay, Mandarin Chinese, Mexican Spanish, Norwegian, Polish, Portuguese, Romanian*, Russian, Spanish, Swedish, Thai, Turkish, Vietnamese
*Book only